MW01287221

WHAT
LOVE
LEFT
Unfinished

ISBN: 978-978-60880-5-1

Published in Nigeria by WORITAL GLOBAL, 2024
6b Lanre Awolokun Street, Gbagada Phase 2, Lagos, Nigeria.
WORITAL (hello@worital.com)
+2348114027024

Cover Design and Interior Layout by:
WORITAL (hello@worital.com)

Printed by
Harmony Publishing
Plot 8, Providence Street, Opposite Halifield School, Lekki Phase 1,
Lagos, Nigeria.
+2347032212481
publish@harmonypublishing.com.ng

DEDICATION

I dedicate this book to God, who has been my source of strength.

To myself, for showing up and pushing through.

For Tobi, who left the earth but lives on in these pages and many people's hearts.

To everyone who finds a piece of themselves in these pages.

FOREWORD

I met Esther in 2015 at Riverside Church in Exeter, and our next contact was in Abuja when she was a law student. Shy and smart, I was always happy to see her. When I saw she had just married, I was excited and asked for her wedding pictures. "What a beautiful couple," I said as I looked through the pictures. So, when a few weeks later she sent me a message saying he was gone, I thought I was dreaming.

It was no dream, and seeing Esther during the different stages after Tobi's loss was humbling. When she started writing on Medium, I was glad as I know firsthand how therapeutic writing can be. When she told me she was writing a book, I was excited and honoured to write the foreword.

Esther's story is filled with love, hope, tragedy, and healing. In her memoir, Esther conveys these emotions and takes you on her journey in her relationship with her beloved Tobi. Each chapter unfolds this love story with joy yet poignancy. Her use of language is simple yet captivating, making you eager to see the love story grow and metamorphose.

I could not put this book down; I am certain most readers will feel the same. Well done, Esther, for unburdening your soul and sharing this story with such honesty. Those who read it will enjoy it and find solace in your words.

"Grief is the price we pay for love" is a quote often attributed to Queen Elizabeth, and it is true. It is also true that we can choose to focus on the pain or the beautiful memories. In this book, Esther fully acknowledges the pain, recognises the importance of healing, and pays tribute to the memories of love and friendship. For in the end, "Love never fails."

– Chioma Momah

REVIEWS

Not everyone believes in love. 'Aromantics' or 'disillusioned romantics' believe that love is overrated. According to such people, love has become a profitable market, moving on from its original noble meaning to a form of make-believe, where it's about who can make their partner happier or who can show off more between two partners.

However, experts confirm that the force of love is one of the most significant influences on earth. This incredible emotion gives us reason to smile and teaches us to look at the brighter side of life. Apart from encouraging empathy, love gives us hope and makes us more patient. It is certainly one of the most beautiful emotions that make our lives worthwhile.

In addition, it is believed that love is more important than money. You work to provide for yourself and your family. Without love, there is little to inspire you to work harder or to have nicer things. There is also no one to whom you can leave the things you have worked hard for in life, and you can't take them with you when you pass away. More importantly, the attraction of a love story is better felt than imagined.

That was exactly how I felt as I read Esther Okuru's beautiful, well-written love story, "What Love Left Unfinished." Written in a lucid first-person narrative, the story takes place in Lagos, Abuja, and Port Harcourt—perhaps Nigeria's three most vibrant and romantic cities.

The book tells the true story of Esther, a young lady who attended a wedding party much against her will. Little did she know that she was going to meet her future husband, Babatobi, at the event. Despite her refusal to dance with the young man— whom she described as 'a tall, strikingly handsome man, with a neatly trimmed beard and an air of confidence about him'—the encounter at the wedding party was the beginning of a blissful relationship that finally culminated in marriage.

Although love is the central theme of the book, nuggets of life and faith are also found in its elegant pages. As Esther put it, "We spoke about faith. He was a Christian, almost certain he was going to be a Pastor, and I was happy with that piece of information. It was pretty rare to find men in Abuja so open about their faith. It made him all the more endearing because he told me of his own volition. I was invested in my faith and glad that he was too. It meant that we could be friends."

Reading this book turns out to be an encounter not only between two lovers but also among an assemblage of friends, family, relatives, and work colleagues who, despite Tobi and Esther's different ethnicities, gave the couple superb support.

The book is a poetic journey of two souls. Despite Tobi's tragic death, it is a curative assemblage of memories of joy, bloom, courage, hopes, and fears. Above all, it is a celebration of life that will deeply resonate with readers of different generations.

Credit must go to the author, who, despite the pain and agony of her husband's death, was still able to put together such a remarkable book full of strong characters, love, and beautiful memories.

- Dr. Wale Okediran
Secretary General, Pan African Writers Association, Accra, Ghana

Art, they say, imitates life. In this must-read tale of incredible love and painful loss, life imitates art. You'll be drawn into a world of heartwarming romance, almost believing it's a fictional realm immune to the harsh realities of loss. Then, grief strikes with a palpable force, reminding you that this is a journey grounded in the rawness of real life. It's a journey of vulnerability, self-discovery, and a breath of hope amidst the stifling fog of grief.

This book is for anyone who has experienced (or is experiencing) nuanced love. Yes, true love exists. It's also for those whom death has left stark and stranded. It's for those hoping to navigate the difficult paths of life after loss. The beautiful writing style makes it an engaging read for almost everyone. But be warned—it's not an easy journey. However, it's undoubtedly a worthy one.

- Obaditan Oluwakorede (OBA.T.K)

Esther Okuru's book is an emotional and compelling journey through love and loss that grips you from the very first page. She shares her story of meeting her husband, the whirlwind romance leading to their marriage, and the heart-wrenching pain of losing him just five weeks after their vows. Her vivid descriptions make you feel as though you are walking beside her through every chapter of her life. Her ability to transport readers into these deeply personal moments is commendable, making the story both relatable and incredibly moving.

What stands out most is how she masterfully balances the themes of love and grief. Her story paints a portrait of true love—its beauty, depth, and transformative power—while also serving as a guide for anyone navigating loss. The raw honesty with which she expresses her emotions and struggles pulls you in, making it impossible to put the book down. The book is gripping, thought-provoking, and deeply touching, leaving you with the sense that love, even in its briefest form, can be everlasting. Esther's journey of healing is inspiring and a testament to the human spirit's ability to endure. This book is a must-read for anyone who has experienced grief or simply believes in the power of love.

- Owajikatelem Ogbuluijah

A vivid and visceral tale. It feels like we were there every step of the way. Simple and powerful, yet touching and engaging. An unfinished symphony of love, grief, and life.

- Dr. Ifeoma Sani

How can I tell you well enough about the gripping content and significance of this well-written testament of love? The book, *"What Love Left Unfinished"* is a testament written by a heartbroken young lady who lost her husband, Tobi Ayo, only five weeks into their marriage. Tobi was a young, brilliant, and ambitious man who loved basketball, and Esther was a pious damsel who was entirely swept off her feet by him. Tobi was the cloud in which she floated, lost in love.

Eagerly, they looked forward to a beautiful future. Still, fate had a totally different idea, snatching Tobi away abruptly and leaving Esther to crash from the sky, shattering all her emotional bones.

What Love Left Unfinished is her heroic attempt to piece those bones together through a heart-twisting tribute to Tobi and the love they shared.

Her book, divided into three parts, describes the course of their love affair in detail. Reading it, you almost feel she was transcribing from a video recording of their brief time together. But of course, she wasn't. Her narrative was pulled from memory, where it was glued by love.

Part One introduces us to how they met, and how their friendship sprouted and blossomed. It tells us how they both began to vibrate like two tuning forks with affection for each other and how they achieved resonance, falling madly in love. It describes how their aura of love expanded to embrace their friends and families.

Destiny had found and joined them as a couple. Love had merged them into one heart with two chambers: one, Tobi, and the other, Esther. They had become inseparable. Esther breathed the expectancy of marriage while Tobi quietly planned it. He executed the first stroke through a surprise party, sealing the glide of an engagement ring onto Esther's finger with the terse statement, "We die here."

Translated for the uninitiated into the Nigerian English space, he meant, "I am in this with you, for better, for worse." By those three words, Tobi meant he was all in, totally committed to the marriage. That was Tobi, a man of passion, as your reading of the book would bear out.

Part Two leads us to the wedding and all the dramatic antecedent scenes in the triangular shuttles between Abuja, Lagos, and Port Harcourt, where it actually took place. Tobi showed himself through Esther's narration as a consummate organizer with an acute sense of detail. Let me illustrate.

Two days before the wedding, Tobi approached the officiating priest to ask him to take a look at his wife's wedding dress specifically. The request initially puzzled the priest. But Tobi wanted to be sure that the dress was in line with the possible guidelines of the church.

Remarkably, when the priest saw the dress, he disapproved of it. Naturally, with only two days to go, Esther was flustered and frustrated. But Tobi was calm, believing there would be a solution. With a cool head, he found one. It was agreed that a jacket be added to Esther's apparel, and that did it.

Part Three of the book tells us about Tobi's ghastly and fatal accident, but also about their honeymoon. The love, the passion, the novelties of a brand new marriage, and their first night as a married couple. It also describes their first daybreak together and how the young man sweetly greeted his wife, still drowsy from sleep, "Good morning, Mrs. Ayo."

Part Three also tells us about how Providence extended its honeymoon. They had just wedded and could not have enough of each other, but Esther had to return to Lagos for work. Reluctantly, they proceeded to the airport for her to catch a flight, only to be told that there would be no flights that day, as the runway was blocked. I leave you to imagine whether the couple minded the gift of one more night for their honeymoon.

"What Love Left Unfinished" clearly announces Esther as a storyteller, even if of one with an autobiographical flavour. But I would be remiss if I did not point out specifically that Esther has given the world a valuable gift through this book. She has shown how to cope with grief and even use its energy to make positive impacts in the lives of others.

She has shown us that writing is an amazing blessing. She has shown how it can be deployed in the darkest moments to survive the pains of tragedy. Esther has demonstrated that writing is therapeutic. This book is evidence. And so is her confession of the relief she felt each time she unburdened herself on an online writing platform. Writing about her pain magically relieved her.

Esther has also shown us that solidarity with mutually impacted grievers can help with collective survival, as with her and her parents-in-law, to whom Tobi was one of only two children. In Esther's words, Tobi's parents "were my anchor, the only thing keeping me grounded." She showed that even in deep pain, grievers should harness opportunities to uplift one another, as we see in the celebration of Tobi's mother's birthday.

To quote her, "We celebrated Tobi's mother's birthday. I surprised her with a cake, and we celebrated even when the tears came. But they were healing tears. Seeing them smile and laugh healed a part of me, too."

Esther has also shown us that in trying to survive the pain of tragedy, we can look to new skills, as she did. She disclosed, "I threw myself into learning French. It was something that required all my focus, something that allowed me to escape, if only for a little while… it was freeing to be in a new space, a new headspace…"

This testament of Esther also reveals how she used the power of the love she shared with her late husband, coupled with imagination, to cope. She wrote, "(Although) Tobi is no longer here in person, he is with me every step of the way. His love surrounds me, his spirit guides me, and his memory strengthens me."

As his memory strengthened her, so did the foundation established in his name reassure her that he lives on. "The foundation we started in his honour is flourishing, funding his basketball players and team, touching lives, just as he did. When I see those boys on the court, I see Tobi in them. I see his passion, drive, and love for the game and life."

Even beyond all these, Esther shows us, by this book, to be grateful for the life of a departed beloved and, in particular, for all the love they gave us while here. It is likely that profuse gratitude would drip through her words onto the palms of those lucky enough to hold her book in their hands.

"I realised," she wrote, "that we had crammed a lifetime of love into the brief time we shared. It was a whirlwind of emotions but also the most beautiful chapter of my life. The love we shared, though brief, was infinite in depth. I am who I am today, because of Tobi."

Because of Tobi, perhaps we all are better versions of ourselves.

- Kudo Eresia-Eke

CONTENTS

PART

ONE

A CHANCE ENCOUNTER

···

Who had a wedding on a Friday?

I grumbled under my breath because there I was, dressed in my work clothes, watching as people trickled in and out of the wedding venue without any interest in a noisy evening. I sat in my car, the soft hum of the engine providing a steady background noise to my thoughts. The air outside was thick with the sticky heat of the early evening, the kind that clung to my skin and made everything feel just a bit more oppressive. I had parked a fair distance from the wedding venue, a grand event hall lit up like a beacon in the twilight. The lights cast a warm, inviting glow across the parking lot.

I sighed, running a hand through my hair, which was pulled back behind my face. My corporate attire—a simple, navy blue blouse paired with black slacks—felt out of place among the Asoebi and sharp suits of the wedding guests. I glanced at my reflection in the rearview mirror, noting the smudges under my eyes from a long week at work and the absence of makeup on my tired face.

"I really should have just gone home," I muttered to myself, drumming my fingers on the steering wheel.

My brother had insisted I come to the wedding, promising it would be a good break from my hectic work schedule. Plus, he'd sounded like he really needed the ride. Yet here I was, underdressed and feeling out of sorts, waiting for him to come out of the hall so I could drive him home.

Through the windscreen, I watched as guests began to walk out of the venue, laughing and chatting, their joy palpable through the glass. Women in vibrant, flowing dresses and men in sleek suits passed by my car. But there was no sign of my brother.

With a sigh of resignation, I unbuckled my seatbelt and stepped out of the car, the sound of my heels clicking against the pavement. I smoothed down my blouse, feeling a pang of self-consciousness as I compared my understated look to the elaborate attire of the other guests. I began to walk towards the entrance, my eyes scanning the crowd for any sign of my brother.

As I approached, I saw a few familiar faces. Old acquaintances from secondary school I hadn't seen in years waved and called out my name.

"Esther, is that you? Ah ah! How are you?"

I forced a smile, pausing to exchange greetings.

"Yes, it's me," I said, trying to keep the conversation brief. "I'm just looking for my brother. He seems to have vanished. Do you know where he is?"

One of my ex-secondary schoolmates, a "senior," a plump lady in a sequined gown, chuckled and patted my arm. "You should be inside, mingling. Young people like you should be having fun, nau."

I laughed lightly. "Maybe," I said, "Maybe it's even here I'll find a husband." I teased, but she nodded seriously.

"By God's grace." She agreed.

I rolled my eyes at her. I should have known better than cracking that particular joke.

A random family friend joined in the laughter, ignoring my exasperation, while my eyes continued to dart around the crowd. It was a good-natured joke, but there was a kernel of truth in it that made my stomach twist. I walked through the aisle, pushing the thoughts of marriage out of my mind. I didn't dwell on it.

As I moved through the clusters of people, nodding politely and exchanging pleasantries, I finally caught sight of my brother near the entrance, engaged in animated conversation with a group of friends. Letting out the breath I didn't realise I'd been holding, I quickened my pace, weaving through the throng of wedding guests so as not to lose him among the crowd.

"Hey!" I called out as I approached, waving to catch his attention.

He turned, a wide grin spreading across his face. "Esther! You finally decided to join the party?"

"More like I'm here to drag you home," I replied with a smile, feeling some of the evening's tension melt away.

"Abeg joor, stay small," he said, dismissively waving his hand. I'm not ready to leave; I'm having fun."

I wanted to argue, to remind him that I was exhausted and had an early meeting the next day, but I knew it would be pointless. Instead, I sighed and scanned the room for a quiet corner where I could wait. A small area near the back of the hall caught my attention, away from the main throng of guests.

Making my way through the crowd, I exchanged polite nods and brief greetings with a few familiar faces. The room was filled with laughter and music, the atmosphere loud and joyous. The decor was stunning, with elaborate flower arrangements and shimmering lights casting a warm glow over everyone.

I dragged a chair to the secluded spot, letting out a deep breath and quickly took my seat quietly in the wedding hall to allow my brother some moments of fun.

Secluded areas are my best spots during public functions because, from my vantage point, I can watch the celebration continue without necessarily participating.

People danced with abandon, their movements fluid and graceful. After a while, I got tired of watching people dance and called a friend, Jojo, who lived close by, to keep me company while I waited. She was happy to oblige so that I wouldn't be alone. We chatted a bit, but our conversation soon became boring, and I resorted to pressing my phone.

Other people like me who were uninterested in the dance gathered in small groups, chatting animatedly and sipping on colourful cocktails. The energy in the room was infectious, but I felt like an outsider looking in.

One cute, smallish, caramel-skinned usher passed by my table and made me glance up from my phone to admire her well-tailored outfit. As soon as I did, I noticed a tall, strikingly handsome man with a neatly trimmed beard and an air of confidence about him approaching my table. He wore the traditional Yoruba male attire, Agbada, a rich shade of white, adorned with intricate embroidery and a coral bead necklace, and he moved with relaxed grace, his eyes scanning the crowd before locking onto mine.

He stopped in front of me and held out his hand. "Would you like to dance?" he asked, his voice deep and warm.

I looked up at him, taking in his tall frame and kind eyes. Despite my exhaustion, I was amused by the situation.

"I'm not really in the mood to dance," I admitted, offering him a small smile. "And even if I was, I can't dance to save my life."

He chuckled, a rich, genuine sound that made me smile wider. "Shey, is this how you're going to find a husband?" He teased, his eyes twinkling with mischief.

I laughed, shaking my head. "Maybe not today," I replied.

He repeated the same question with renewed vigour, a wide grin spreading across his face, and laughed. It was a rich, deep sound that made me smile despite myself. "Shey, this is how you're going to find a husband?" he teased, his eyes twinkling with amusement.

I shook my head in affirmation, unable to suppress a grin.

"Fair enough," he said with a playful grin. "But remember, practice makes perfect."

He gave me a slight bow and walked off to rejoin the dancers. I watched him go, feeling a strange mix of amusement and curiosity. Despite the evening's weariness, our brief encounter had lifted my spirits.

I sat there in my little corner and watched him dance, his movements graceful and confident, before he returned to my side.

"Still not in the mood to dance?" he asked, his smile wider this time.

I laughed genuinely this time. "Don't you have anyone else to dance with?" I asked, raising an eyebrow. "I'm sure there are plenty of willing partners."

He shrugged, leaning casually against the wall. "I want to dance with you," he insisted. His tone was playful but earnest.

I shook my head again, more firmly this time. "No, really. I'm not much of a dancer."

He laughed again, the sound infectious. "Well, if you change your mind, I'll be right here," he said, giving me a mock salute before walking off to rejoin the dancers.

I watched him go, intrigued despite myself. Who was this man, and why was he so insistent on dancing with me? I was impressed by his persistence and easy charm. I wondered what kind of person he was and why he had singled me out in a room full of people. He turned once again and caught my frown in his direction. He responded with a cheeky grin and a wink, which deepened my intrigue.

As the night progressed, the energy in the hall only seemed to heighten. The music grew louder, the laughter more infectious, and the dancing more exuberant. As I'd heard someone call him, Tobi danced badly to a few more songs, but people gravitated towards him, drawn by his charisma, ease, and ability not to take himself too seriously.

I found myself watching him more than I cared to admit, my gaze following his every move. He was like a magnet, and even though I tried to remain indifferent, something about his energy was mesmerising.

The day dragged on, and I soon lost track of time and my desire to return home for peace and quietness.

The after-party was in full swing when he found me again in my little corner. I was still sitting, trying to blend into the background while the celebration continued around me.

"Ah, you're still sitting here," he teased, his eyes twinkling with amusement.

I shrugged, offering him a small smile. "Some of us are better suited to people-watching."

He chuckled and shook his head. "If you don't want to dance with me, I'll sit and talk with you instead."

"You don't have to," I protested, though I couldn't hide the warmth spreading through me at his offer.

He waved away my protests with a dismissive hand and shot me a smile that made my heart flutter unexpectedly. "I insist."

There was something about his smile that was contagious, and I found myself smiling back at him. "If you insist," I agreed, unable to hide my amusement.

He pulled a chair next to mine and sat down, the two of us slightly removed from the bustling dance floor. We sat in comfortable silence for a moment, watching the scene before us.

"Why are you sitting here all alone?" he asked, turning his attention fully to me. His gaze was intense but not intimidating; it seemed more like he was genuinely interested in my answer.

I shrugged, feeling a bit self-conscious. "I'm not really in the mood for dancing. And, honestly, I'm not very good at it."

He laughed softly. "Not everyone has to be good at dancing. It's more about enjoying the moment."

I raised an eyebrow. "And you seem to enjoy it a lot."

He grinned. "I do. But there's more to a good party than just dancing."

"Like what?" I asked, curious.

"Like good conversation," he replied, his eyes twinkling with mischief. "And getting to know interesting people."

I felt a blush creeping up my cheeks. "I wouldn't say I'm interesting."

He leaned back in his chair, studying me thoughtfully. "I think you are. Anyone who can sit alone at a wedding and not feel the need to fit in must have some interesting thoughts."

I laughed, feeling more at ease. "Maybe. Or maybe I'm just tired."

"Tired of what?" he asked gently.

"Work. Life. Expectations," I admitted, surprised at how easily the words came out.

He nodded, his expression empathetic. "I get that. Sometimes, it's good to take a break from it all. Even if it's just for a few hours at a wedding."

I looked at him, really looked at him, and saw more than just the charming random man. There was depth in his eyes, an unexpected kindness. "You make it sound so simple."

He smiled softly. "Sometimes, it is. Sometimes, you just need to let go and live in the moment."

LOVE BLOOM IN THE GARDEN OF FRIENDSHIP

As the night went on, the high-energy atmosphere around us seemed to fade into the background. The music and laughter became a distant hum, and it felt like we were in our little world. The chemistry between us was undeniable, and I found myself more drawn to his warmth and sincerity.

He leaned back into his seat and smiled. I grinned back and relaxed in my seat.

"So Esther, what do you like to do besides not dancing at weddings?"

I responded to him with a quiet smile. We kept people-watching while the day dragged on into the night.

Instead of feeling impatient about my brother's involvement in the wedding festivities, I found myself appreciating the moment, sitting next to Tobi. There was a calmness in our conversation that felt natural, almost as if we had been friends for years. It was easy and comfortable.

"So, what do you do when you're not people-watching at weddings?" he asked teasingly.

I laughed. "Well, I actually enjoy going to the gym. It's my escape from the stress of work and life."

"Really?" His eyes lit up with genuine interest. "I'm passionate about basketball. I even coach a local team."

"That's impressive!" I said, feeling genuine admiration for him. "I've always admired people who can play indoor and outdoor games well. All that jumping must be a lot of work."

He chuckled. "It's not as hard as it looks. Maybe you should come to one of our games sometime. I'll even give you a few pointers."

I smiled, enjoying the easy banter. "I'd like that. But you have to promise not to laugh when I miss a shot or ten."

"No promises," he laughed. "So, what else do you like to do for fun?"

"I love exploring new places, especially restaurants," I admitted.

"I used to go with a friend, but she moved away recently. Now, I just go alone."

"That sounds like fun," he said thoughtfully. "I never really go anywhere. Maybe I could be your new partner. You can show me all the cool spots in Abuja."

I grinned. "Deal. But you have to agree to be adventurous. No picky eaters allowed."

"Deal," he agreed, holding his hand for a shake.

We chatted for hours, our conversation flowing effortlessly from one topic to another. We discussed everything from our favourite books and movies to our childhood memories and his trip to Korea. He'd just recently come back, and I was fascinated by his tales of travelling. I had always wanted to explore the world myself, but in this country, travelling was a lot harder than it should have been.

We spoke about faith. He was a Christian, almost certain he would be a pastor, and I was happy at that information. It was rare to find men in Abuja so open about their faith. It made him all the more endearing because he told me of his volition. I was invested in my faith and glad that he was, too. It meant that we could be friends.

Our little moment felt like we were the only two people in the room, the rest of the world fading into the background.

As the after-party wound down and cleaners started to move in, I realised how much time had passed. Decorators began setting up for another wedding happening in the same hall the next day. The night had flown by in a blur of laughter and easy conversation. I found that both of us were lingering over the conversation, not wanting it to end. But as the noise from the decorators became louder, it became more difficult to hear each other. Our special moment was interrupted, and I stirred.

Tobi glanced around, too, noticing the activity. "Looks like it's time to go."

"Yeah," I said, feeling a twinge of sadness at the thought of our night ending. "I had a great time."

"Me too," he said, standing up and stretching. "It's been a while since I've enjoyed a wedding this much."

I realised then that Tobi hadn't asked for my number. I didn't want to let this connection slip away.

"Hey, can I get your number? I think it would be fun to introduce you to some great spots in Abuja. You're a great company, after all."

He smiled, clearly pleased. "Of course."

I quickly typed his number. "I'm looking forward to our adventures."

"Me too," he said, his smile warm and genuine. "See you soon, Esther."

As we walked out of the hall together, I felt a sense of excitement and anticipation. This night had been unexpected, but it felt like the beginning of something wonderful. I strongly believe it is a chance encounter. And while I wasn't thinking of romance just yet, I knew that Tobi and I had the potential to become great friends. The future suddenly seemed a little brighter. He walked me to my car and went off in search of his own. I waited for my brother to wrap up his conversations, and we went home together.

As I settled in to sleep off the day, I could not help but chuckle at how my day went. It was funny that a few hours ago, I was annoyed by my brother's intrusion into my day because of his insistence that we attend the wedding party together, despite knowing how tasking my day went. But now, all of that lingering annoyance is gone. I smiled to bed like a newborn baby.

The following day, I saw Tobi again at a mutual friend's get-together. It was a casual affair, just a few friends hanging out and catching up. We exchanged a brief greeting, nothing more. There were no lingering glances or meaningful conversations, just a simple "hello" in passing. It was as if we were both giving each other space, letting the night before settle into our minds without rushing into anything new.

A week later, I found myself thinking about him. On a whim, I sent him a message on WhatsApp to check up on him.

"Hey Tobi, how's it going?" I typed, wondering if he would even remember me.

His reply came quickly. "Hey Esther, I'm good. How about you?"

"Good, just busy with work," I replied, keeping it light.

"Yeah, I hear you. Same here," he said, and the conversation naturally came to a close after a few more exchanges. It was brief but pleasant, enough to keep the connection alive without feeling forced.

Another week passed before I received a message from Tobi. "Hey Esther, how's your week going?" he asked.

I smiled at the screen before typing back. "Pretty good, thanks! How about you?"

"Not bad. I was thinking that we should continue our conversation over lunch. What do you think?" he replied.

I hesitated for a moment, then typed, "That sounds like a great idea. How about Friday?"

"Perfect. Do you have a place in mind?" he asked.

"Yes, there's a poolside restaurant attached to a boutique hotel that I think you'll like. It's got a great vibe," I suggested.

"Sounds perfect. Looking forward to it," he replied.

The bright morning sun heralded our long-awaited Friday hangout. I chose to wear a casual yet classy outfit, wanting to feel comfortable and confident at the same time. The poolside restaurant was as charming as I remembered, with its relaxed atmosphere and beautiful view of the water. I arrived a few minutes early to steal a moment to appreciate the setting by myself.

Tobi arrived shortly after, on time, dressed in a casual button-down shirt and jeans. His smile was warm and genuine, instantly putting me at ease.

"Esther, this place is amazing," he said as we settled into our seats.

"I'm glad you like it," I replied, feeling a sense of satisfaction at his approval.

As we looked over the menu, Tobi began to share stories of his time in Korea. "I spent a few months there. It's fascinating how different yet alike we all are," he said. The culture is so different from ours. It's fascinating."

"Tell me more," I urged, genuinely curious.

He launched into tales of his experiences, from the food to the people and the unexpected challenges he faced.

"One of my funniest moments there was trying to find my way in the subway system. Everything was in Korean, and I got lost so many times," he said with a laugh.

I laughed along with him, picturing him in those situations. "I can imagine! It must have been quite the adventure."

"It was," he agreed. "But it also taught me many important things to know about adapting to new environments and people from all walks of life."

As we chatted, I found myself increasingly intrigued by his stories. He had a way of making even the mundane sound exciting. His passion for basketball came up again, and he told me about the local team he coached. "It's rewarding to see the kids improve and develop a love for the game," he said, his eyes lighting up.

Our food arrived, and we enjoyed both the meal and the conversation. Just as I was about to ask him another question, his phone rang. He glanced at the screen and smiled slightly. "It's my dad," he said, excusing himself to take the call.

"Good evening, sir," he said, his voice warm. "I'm out right now... with a friend. Her name is Esther, but you don't know her."

I couldn't hear his father's response, but Tobi's expression softened into a smile. "Sure, hang on," he said, handing me the phone. "He wants to speak with you."

Surprised, I took the phone. "Good evening, Sir?"

"Hello, Esther. How are you? I hear you are out with my son. I just wanted to make sure my son is safe with you," his father said, his tone playful yet sincere.

I laughed. "Yes, Sir. He's in good hands."

"That's good to hear. Take care of him for me," he said before we exchanged goodbyes, and I returned the phone to Tobi.

"Your dad is cool," I said, still smiling.

Tobi chuckled. "Yeah, he's something else. Just don't mind."

"No need to apologise. It was sweet," I said, feeling the stirrings of a deeper connection. I liked his father; from that brief conversation, I could tell that they were very alike.

As we continued our lunch, the conversation flowed easily. There was no rush, just a slow and steady rhythm of getting to know each other. We spoke about our families, our aspirations, and even our fears. It was refreshing to have someone listen and share so openly. After finishing our meal, we decided to explore the rooftop of the boutique hotel, curious to see the view. The rooftop was serene, offering a panoramic view of the city. Tobi pulled out his phone and began taking pictures of the skyline. Then, he turned the camera on me, snapping candid shots as I smiled and laughed. I felt a sense of lightness, the evening breeze playing with my hair as Tobi captured those moments

"Don't worry; I have appointed myself your Abuja tour guide. We will be back here."

By the time we were ready to leave, the sun was beginning to set, casting a warm evening glow over the pool. I realised that I was looking forward to our next meeting, eager to learn more about this intriguing man who had unexpectedly come into my life.

"Thank you for today," I said as we walked to our cars.

"Thank you, Esther. I had a great time," he replied, his smile reflecting my feelings.

This time, I knew we would keep in touch more regularly. As I drove home, I felt this was the beginning of something special, like the dandelion leaves in winter. Only time would tell whether it was a deep friendship or something more. But for now, I was content to enjoy the promise of an adventure on this journey, one slow, meaningful step at a time.

I found it hard to sleep that night, my mind replaying the evening's events. The warmth of Tobi's smile and his genuine interest in our conversation kept returning to me. I couldn't help but smile as I thought about our plans to explore the city together. It felt like the start of a beautiful friendship. Eventually, I drifted off with thoughts of our laughter and shared stories.

WHAT LOVE LEFT UNFINISHED

ONE RHYTHM, TWO SOULS

....

It takes two to tango.

The next morning, I awoke to the soft glow of dawn spilling through the curtains, gently nudging me from my dreams. The air was crisp with the freshness of a new day, and I could hear the sweet melody of birds singing outside my window; their song carried on a cool, invigorating breeze. The rustling of leaves seemed to echo the quiet optimism that filled me. Stretching, I rolled out of bed, feeling unusually light-hearted, as if the joy from last night had followed me into the morning.

As I reached for my phone, a message from Tobi popped up on the screen. "Hey, Esther! How about we meet up again soon? You still owe me a dance from the wedding, remember? Better bring your dancing shoes this time."

I chuckled and replied, "Tobi, I already told you I don't know how to dance, and I don't even have dancing shoes."

Within seconds, his response pinged back. "Pick a place with music, anyway. Music needs no permission to take effect on one's soul. I'll handle the rest."

Rolling my eyes, I texted back, "Fine, fine. I'll pick a random place, but don't stress me about dancing!"

Later that day, I found a quaint café without music and sent Tobi the details. He immediately called me.

"Esther, I said a place with music! How am I supposed to get you to dance without music?" His voice was light, teasing.

I sighed, "Alright, alright. I'll find another place."

Later that evening, we sat across from each other in the quaint café I had chosen. It was peaceful, quiet, and completely devoid of any music. We laughed and chatted over coffee, and I promised that next time, I'd find a spot with music just like he'd asked.

We made plans for our next meeting, and as I thought about the promise I had made to him, I couldn't help but smile. I realised that spending time with Tobi felt both exciting and meaningful, like a friendship I hadn't realised I'd been missing.

The day of our next meeting arrived quickly. I had chosen a trendy bar this time, one where the music blared through the walls and the energy was electric. When we stepped inside, Tobi and I shared a look and immediately burst into laughter. The noise was overwhelming, and it was clear neither of us felt comfortable there.

Tobi leaned in close, his breath warm against my ear as he shouted over the music, "I think we might have made a mistake."

I nodded vigorously. "Yeah, let's get out of here."

We escaped to a quieter café nearby, one with cosy seating and soft background music that allowed for easy conversation. We both let out relieved sighs, the breath we didn't realise we were holding.

"Much better," I said, smiling at Tobi.

"Agreed," he replied, shaking his head with a grin. "I'm unsure what I thought about the whole dancing idea."

We spent the rest of the evening chatting about everything and nothing. The conversation flowed effortlessly, and I found myself losing track of time. By the end of the night, we both knew it wouldn't be the last time we saw each other.

We met up again the following weekend and then the weekend after that. Our weekends quickly became regular hangouts, and we both looked forward to our special moments.

One evening after work, I found myself dialling Tobi's number as I sat in traffic. "Hey, Tobi. I'm in the neighbourhood. Would you mind if I stopped by?"

"Sure thing, Esther. Come on over."

The truth was, I wasn't really in the neighbourhood—I just wanted to see him. I parked outside his house, and we ended up chatting in my car for hours. We shared stories, dreams, and fears, the conversation only ending when the mosquitoes became unbearable.

"Alright, I think we're being eaten alive," Tobi laughed, swatting at his arm. "Time to call it a night."

I nodded, reluctantly starting my car. "Same time tomorrow?"

He grinned. "You bet."

This became our routine. Every evening, I'd call Tobi on my way home, and we'd spend hours talking in my car until the night grew late and the mosquitoes drove us apart. Each night, it felt like we were building something magical, though we wanted to avoid rushing or defining it too soon.

One evening, as we sat in the car with the streetlights casting a soft glow over us, Tobi turned to me with a serious expression. "You know, Esther, I really enjoy these talks. I feel like I can be myself with you."

I smiled, feeling a warmth spread through me. "I feel the same way, Tobi. It's like we've known each other forever."

He reached out, giving my hand a gentle squeeze. "I'm glad we met."

"Me too," I replied, squeezing back.

As we were deep in conversation, Tobi's dad called to tell him we should come inside.

"You two, come into the house; I don't think it's very safe for you people to be sitting outside in the car so late." I could hear him say.

I glanced at Tobi, who shrugged and smiled. "I guess we should listen to him."

We gathered our things and went inside. The house was warm and inviting, filled with the comforting smells of dinner and the sounds of family chatter. Over the next few meetings, Tobi and I started taking his dad's suggestion seriously. It became our new norm to hang out inside the house rather than in my car.

Tobi's family was welcoming. Despite my protests that I'd already eaten, his mother always offered me food. His younger sister, Temi, quickly became my friend. We'd chat about everything from school to fashion, and I found myself looking forward to seeing her as much as I did Tobi.

When March rolled around, I no longer needed to call Tobi when I arrived. I'd just let myself into the compound, greeted by his family's familiar smiles. One evening, after a particularly long day at work, I walked in and flopped onto the couch beside his sister.

"Rough day?" she asked, handing me a glass of cold water.

"You have no idea," I groaned, grateful for the refreshment.

Tobi came in a few minutes later, his usual grin lighting up his face. "Hey, Esther! Good to see you survived another day in the corporate jungle."

I rolled my eyes. "Barely."

Over the next few weeks, my bond with Tobi's family grew stronger. His mom started treating me like one of her own, always ensuring I had enough to eat and asking about my day. His dad frequently asked for my opinion on the news of the day, valuing my perspective in a way that made me feel respected and valued. It was like finding a second home, a place where I felt completely at ease.

Tobi and I spent nearly all our free time together. We started going to flag football games every Sunday, a ritual that quickly became the best part of my week. At first, I was just a spectator, cheering him on from the sidelines, but soon, I found myself getting involved, learning the rules, and even tossing the ball around with him and his friends.

His friends and family became so accustomed to our constant companionship that if they couldn't reach Tobi, they would call me to ask if I was with him. It became a running joke that wherever one of us was, the other wasn't far behind. I didn't mind; I enjoyed his company, and Tobi never made me question whether or not he wanted my company.

In early April, Tobi and I were sitting in my car, talking as usual. During a lull, he turned to me with a thoughtful expression and said, "Esther, have you ever thought about living abroad?"

I raised an eyebrow, surprised by the sudden change in topic. "Not really. Why do you ask?"

He shrugged, trying to appear nonchalant. "I was just thinking... What if you had to move? Like, say, to Canada?"

I knew he was applying for permanent residency in Canada. He had mentioned it before, but it was always in a distant, hypothetical context. This felt different, more personal.

"Canada, huh?" I mused, trying to keep my tone light. "It would be a big change. But why the sudden interest?"

Tobi looked at me, his eyes serious. "Just wondering. You know, in case I end up there. Would you ever consider it?"

I felt a flutter of something in my chest, something I didn't want to name just yet. "I guess it would depend on a lot of things," I replied cautiously. "But I wouldn't rule it out."

He nodded, seeming satisfied with my answer, and turned back to the game. But the conversation lingered in my mind long after.

As we continued our conversation, Tobi turned to me again with a thoughtful look. "What do you think about being a pastor's wife, Esther?"

I blinked, taken aback. "A pastor's wife? Why do you ask?"

He shrugged, but there was a seriousness in his eyes. "Just curious. You know how much I love God, and it's always been a big part of my life. I've been thinking about the future a lot lately."

I felt a flutter in my chest again, stronger this time. "Well, it's a big responsibility," I said slowly, choosing my words carefully. "Supporting your spouse in their ministry, being a part of the community... It's a lot to consider."

Tobi nodded. "Yeah, it is. But it's also rewarding, I think. Being part of something bigger than yourself."

I nodded. Was he hinting at something more? Over the past few months, we'd grown so close, spending almost every weekend together and countless hours on the phone.

"I suppose it would be," I said softly. "But it would depend on a lot of things, like you said about Canada. It's hard to know until you're in that situation."

He smiled, a small, knowing smile that made my heart skip a beat. "True. It's all about timing and the right circumstances."

I wondered if this was his way of gauging my feelings, of seeing if I was open to something more. The thought both thrilled and terrified me. We continued watching the game, but my mind was distracted.

The rest of the evening passed in a comfortable silence, but my mind kept returning to our conversation. What did it mean for us? Were we crossing into new territory, or was it just idle speculation?

When it was time to leave, Tobi walked me to my car. "Thanks for coming by, Esther. I always enjoy our time together."

"Me too, Tobi," I replied, my voice tinged with an emotion I couldn't quite name. "See you soon?"

"Definitely," he said with a smile.

As I drove home, I suspected that something was shifting between us, that we were on the brink of something new and significant. The future was uncertain, but I was ready to face it, one slow, meaningful step at a time, with Tobi by my side, no matter where life took us.

As June rolled around, I couldn't ignore our growing bond. There was an undeniable connection, even if we hadn't defined it beyond friendship. Our interactions were filled with easy banter and deep conversations, and it was a comforting rhythm. But we both knew unspoken feelings were hovering just beneath the surface.

MORE THAN WORDS

As we sat outside under the stars again one evening, my phone buzzed with a notification. I glanced at the screen and felt my stomach drop. It was an email from a company in Lagos, offering me a job I'd applied for months ago and had completely forgotten about.

"Tobi," I said slowly, "I just got a job offer in Lagos."

He looked at me, his expression unreadable. "Are you going to take it?"

"I don't know," I admitted. "It's a great opportunity, but..."

"But?"

"But it means leaving all of this," I gestured around me, to the house, to him.

He was silent for a moment, then he reached out and took my hand. "Whatever you decide, Esther, just know I'll support you."

The warmth of his hand in mine felt sweet. Driving home that night, my mind was a whirlwind of thoughts and emotions. I knew I had a decision to make, one that would shape the course of my future. And for the first time, I acknowledged that my feelings for Tobi were deeper than friendship.

The next few days were a blur. I weighed the pros and cons, spoke to my family, and finally made a decision. I called Tobi one evening, my heart pounding in my chest.

"Tobi, I've decided to take the job in Lagos."

There was a brief silence on the other end of the line. "Really? That's great news!" Tobi's voice was full of excitement.

"But," I quickly added, "this doesn't mean the end for us. I want us to be friends, even if it's long-distance."

Tobi chuckled, clearly enjoying the moment. "Oh, come on, Esther. It's not like you're moving abroad or anything. Lagos is just an hour away by flight. We'll figure it out. You never walk alone," he assured me of his commitment with the slogan of Liverpool, the English football club.

As I hung up the phone, I felt excitement and fear.

That summer brought us closer in ways I hadn't imagined. With my resignation handed in and my leave approved, I suddenly had time—time to explore new places, try out more restaurants, and, most importantly, spend more time with Tobi. We visited every corner of the city, savouring our moments together.

When it came time to prepare for my relocation to Lagos, Tobi was there as usual. He insisted on helping me pack, and thank God he did because his sense of organisation was immaculate. I would have been completely lost without his help. He started with the wardrobe, pulling out my clothes, folding each item, and stacking them neatly in boxes. I stood beside him, trying to keep up, but quickly found myself falling behind.

"How do you do this so fast?" I laughed while struggling to match his pace.

He chuckled, not missing a beat, as he carefully folded my favourite dress. "Years of practice," he said, winking. "Besides, I'm not about to let you leave Lagos without everything perfectly in place."

Then, just three days before my move, he pulled off the most unexpected surprise for my birthday. I walked into a room filled with balloons—all in my favourite colours, black and lilac—and a carefully curated basket that included all the little things he knew I loved. The thoughtfulness of it all and the attention to detail took my breath away. That day, I knew for sure. He had taken the time to understand every small thing that made me happy, and in doing so, he had sealed his place in my heart.

By the time I was ready to move to Lagos, Tobi had packed a lifetime of memories for me to go with. It didn't make missing him any easier. I was already counting down to returning to Abuja to see him before stepping out of the city. We spoke every day, but it wasn't the same as pulling up to his house on my way home.

One weekend in October, I decided to surprise Tobi with a visit. I didn't tell him I was coming, wanting to see the look on his face when I showed up unannounced. As the plane touched down in Abuja, my heart pounded with excitement. I could hardly wait to see him.

After landing in Abuja, I arranged for a friend to pick me up from the airport. To my utter surprise, when I got into the car, Tobi suddenly appeared from the side.

"Surprise!" he said with a wide grin, clearly enjoying my shock.

"How did you...?" I started, but he just winked and gestured for me to get in.

"It was a bit of a covert operation," he explained as we drove to his office. "I reached out to your friend, and we made a plan. I wanted to see you before you headed to Port Harcourt."

At his office, I quickly stashed my things in his car, and we headed to his place. The drive was filled with laughter and catching up. When we arrived at his home, it felt like no time had passed since we last saw each other. We spent the weekend exploring our favourite spots, reminiscing about old times, and creating new memories. We laughed until our sides hurt and spoke about everything and nothing, just like we always did.

On my last day, we found ourselves back at the rooftop where he had taken those pictures of me months ago. The view of Abuja sprawled out beneath us, bathed in the golden light of the setting sun.

"I'm really glad you came," Tobi said, leaning against the railing.

"Me too," I replied, looking at him. "This has been... perfect."

He smiled with a hint of sadness clouding his gaze. "I wish you didn't have to go back so soon."

"I know," I sighed. "But Lagos is where the job is. And you said you'd visit in December, remember?"

He nodded. "I haven't forgotten. I'll be there, by God's grace."

We stood in silence for a moment, the evening settling around us. I turned to him and said, "Tobi, thank you for today. It really means a lot."

"It means a lot to me too, Esther," he replied softly. "And December isn't that far away."

The following day, Tobi drove me to the airport. As we approached the departure terminal, he reached over and squeezed my hand. "Safe flight, Esther. I'll miss you."

"I'll miss you too," I said, trying to keep my voice steady. "See you in December."

He helped me with my bags, and we hugged tightly before I headed inside. As I walked away, I glanced back and saw him standing there, watching me with a bittersweet smile. I waved, and he waved back.

I began desperately yearning for his presence the moment I boarded because we could only spend the previous evening together, since I needed to be in Port Harcourt for my brother's wedding. We did not have enough time to enjoy many evenings together because of my short stay in Abuja. We had gone to the basketball court to surprise his dad. His dad's reaction was priceless—he was overjoyed and told me how much they all missed me in Abuja. It was a perfect, unexpected end to a wonderful visit.

As I settled into my seat on the plane, I replayed the day before in my mind. It had been everything I needed and more. And even though leaving was hard, I felt hopeful about the future.

December would come soon enough, and with it, the hope of another visit, another chance to be together.

I was leaving, but I wasn't really saying goodbye. Our friendship was strong, and I knew that no matter the distance, we would always find our way back to each other. I remembered before I met Tobi, I didn't think I could ever do long distance with anyone. Well, I guess in a way it was great that we hadn't quite defined the relationship, though, in truth, it did matter to me.

WHAT LOVE LEFT UNFINISHED

SPOKEN WORDS

....

I love December.

Whe n Tobi visited Lagos in December, the city was in full festive cheer. The streets on the island were lit up with Christmas lights, and everyone had a Christmas promo going on. The streets were adorned with the usual rowdiness, and a warm, joyous energy filled the air. Or could those be the butterflies in my belly at seeing Tobi again?

We spent the time exploring all the restaurants I wanted to take him to, sampling local delicacies, and enjoying the holiday atmosphere. As the evening approached, we found ourselves in a quieter street, the city's noise fading into the background.

"Tobi, it's really great to have you here," I said, smiling at him. "Lagos is going to be much more fun with you around."

He grinned. "I'm glad to be here. It's been too long since we hung out in person. I've missed those evening hangouts at my place."

It was Tobi's first time meeting with other members of my family living in Lagos. He and my brother already knew each other from school, but it was the first time he met my sister and her husband. In turn, I also met his Grandma, affectionately known as "Mummy Omole," and a few of his aunts and uncles. Though we kept things casual, just as friends to avoid any awkward questions about marriage timelines, meeting Mummy Omole was especially important to Tobi. It was clear how much she meant to him, and it felt significant to be introduced to her, even if just as a friend. In spite of the family visits, we made time for each other, too.

While taking a stroll one evening, Tobi turned to me, his expression suddenly serious. "Esther, I've been thinking a lot about us."

I raised an eyebrow, curious about where this was heading. "Oh? What about us?"

He reached out, taking my hand in his. "Esther, I want to marry you. In April."

I burst into laughter, the absurdity of his statement catching me off guard. "Tobi, I don't know what kind of marriage you're thinking about. You haven't even proposed, haven't met my family in that capacity—nothing. Is that how people get married these days?"

He chuckled, squeezing my hand gently. "I knew you'd say that. But I mean it, Esther. I want to spend the rest of my life with you. You'll see. I'll do everything properly."

"Toh! If you say so, oh." I laughed, but the glint in his eyes told me he was dead serious. I walked away from him, hoping the cool breeze of the air-conditioned beach house would calm my flushed face and racing heart. He followed behind.

He tilted his head, studying my face. "Do you doubt me?"

I laughed some more, trying to brush off the seriousness of his words. "I don't think you're serious, Tobi. Marriage is a big deal, and we haven't even defined what we are. We're friends, remember?"

He shook his head. "I am serious, Esther. I know what I want. Maybe you don't see it now, but I do."

I felt a flutter of excitement in my chest. "April is so soon, Tobi," I said with a small laugh, feeling the sea breeze through my hair. We were on the beach, waiting for my sister, her family, my brother, his wife, and other friends to join us. The fact that it was Christmas Eve added a bit of magic to the moment. The waves crashed against the shore rhythmically, and the cool sea air was a welcome reprieve from the warmth spreading through my cheeks.

He stepped closer, his gaze never wavering. "I know it's soon, but when you know, you know," he said with a grin. "And I've known for a while now. We've both known."

I smiled. It was true; we had always felt it. There was this understanding that we would end up together. We had talked about our futures, weaving each other into our plans. "I mean yes, but Tobi," I said, a teasing note in my voice. April? That's only a few months away. We need more time to plan things properly."

He chuckled softly. "You know me, I'm always ready," he said. "And I know you are too. I've spent enough time with you to know that you're the one I want. It's just a matter of when, not if."

I looked out at the ocean, the waves shimmering under the fading light. He was right—we had known this was where we were headed. "I guess I just didn't expect it to be this soon," I admitted, turning back to him with a soft smile. "But yes, Tobi. I want this too. I want us."

He reached for my hand, his grip firm and reassuring. "Then let's do it," he said, his voice certain. Let's start planning, one step at a time. There's no rush, no pressure, just us moving forward together."

I nodded. There was no doubt, no hesitation. Just the two of us, standing on the cusp of a future we both wanted. "Okay," I agreed, my smile growing wider. "Let's do it."

The rest of the holiday passed in the shared meals, and late-night conversations. We went to the beach, explored the bustling markets, and enjoyed the Christmas holiday together. Every moment with him was filled with a sense of connection that was hard to ignore.

On the last day of his visit, we found ourselves sitting on the balcony, watching the sun set over the city. The sky was a canvas of oranges and pinks, and the air was filled with the sounds of Lagos winding down for the night.

"I don't want to leave," Tobi said, breaking the comfortable silence.

I sighed, feeling a pang of sadness. "I don't want you to go either. It's been so nice having you here."

He reached over and took my hand, his touch warm and reassuring. "I'll come back soon. And remember what I said. I'm serious about us."

I tried to smile, but the thought of him leaving made it hard. "We'll see, Tobi. We'll see."

When it was finally time for him to leave, I dropped him off at the airport, neither of us wanting to say goodbye. He pulled me into a tight hug, his arms wrapping around me in a way that made me feel safe and cherished.

"Take care of yourself," he whispered into my hair.

"You too," I replied, my voice choking with emotion. "Safe travels."

He pulled back slightly, looking into my eyes. "I'll be back before you know it."

I nodded, unable to find the words. As he walked away, a confused mix of emotions swirled inside me. I began the drive back to the office.

After he left, I threw myself into work, trying to distract myself from the emptiness I felt. But no matter how busy I was, thoughts of him kept creeping in. His laugh, his smile, the way he made me feel like I was the only person in the room—his words stayed in my mind.

That evening, as I sat on the couch scrolling through photos from his visit, my phone buzzed with a message. It was from Tobi.

"Hey, just wanted to let you know I got home safely. Missing you already."

I smiled, my heart warming at his words. "Miss you too. The house feels empty without you."

His reply was instant. "It won't be empty for long. I'm already planning my next trip." He teased me. I smiled at my phone screen.

As the weeks passed, our conversations continued, filled with jokes, updates, and the severe occasional talk about the future. Tobi's belief in us started to chip away at my worries that we wouldn't be able to do everything in time. I trusted God that we would.

WHAT LOVE LEFT UNFINISHED

A PROMISE
IN APRIL

*A*pril *was only four months away, and despite knowing deep down that Tobi was the man I wanted to spend the rest of my life with, I questioned whether such a short commitment was feasible.*

Tobi had yet to propose officially, and the uncertainty gnawed at me. By the first week of January, I decided I needed a break from the chaos of Lagos for my mental health, and more importantly, I wanted to see Tobi. I was going to relax, wondering if he would propose and take my mind off it entirely. We were great friends; we texted and spoke every day.

The thought of seeing him again sent butterflies fluttering in my stomach. By the first week of January, I had booked a flight for the first week of February and shrugged my shoulders as the confirmation email for the ticket was sent. The cards would fall where they would, and I trusted that we were on the right path.

When I told Tobi about my flight, he immediately started a countdown on WhatsApp, marking off the days. His enthusiasm was infectious; every day, he sent me little messages that made me smile. A week before my trip, he sent me a detailed itinerary of what we'd be doing during my stay in Abuja. It was meticulously planned, with morning, afternoon, and evening activities all weekend. The amount of attention he had put into it showed. He wanted to take me to all my favourite restaurants and places. The thought of just how well he knew me made me smile.

The day of my flight arrived, and as I boarded the plane, my heart raced with anticipation. The flight seemed to be the slowest in existence, each passing minute heightening my excitement. When we finally touched down in Abuja, I quickly grabbed my bags and hurried to the arrivals area, my eyes scanning the crowd for Tobi.

And there he was, holding his phone up, videoing my arrival. He had a wide grin on his face as he walked toward me. "Ms. Okuru, welcome to Abuja!" he called, and I grinned at him, resisting the urge to launch myself into his arms.

I laughed, feeling giddy and a little embarrassed by his public display. "Tobi, stop it!" I said, trying to swat the phone out of his hand, but he dodged my attempts, still filming.

He finally lowered the phone and pulled me into a tight hug. "I've missed you," whispering in my ear, his embrace making me feel safe and cherished.

"I've missed you too," I replied, my voice muffled against his shoulder. We stood there for a moment, just holding each other, the rest of the world fading away.

Tobi took my bags and led me to the car. "I've got a whole weekend planned for us," he said, his excitement palpable. "First stop, breakfast at your favourite place!"

As we drove through the city, I stole glances at him. The familiar streets of Abuja brought back so many memories of our time together. When we arrived at the restaurant, nostalgia threatened to overwhelm me. But to our disappointment, it was closed. My early flight had landed us here before they had even opened their doors.

Tobi looked at me, a playful glint in his eyes. "No worries. I've got a backup plan. Let's head to your second favourite place, Hytaste."

We drove to another cosy spot, and as we sat down to eat, I felt such gratitude for this man who knew me so well. He ordered my favourite dishes, and we spent the meal catching up, laughing, and simply enjoying each other's company.

After breakfast, we stopped for lunch. My heart was full, so I took the food in a takeaway bag.

"It's so you don't stress about what to eat when you've only just come." He said. As we walked to the car, he kept stealing glances in my direction.

"Why do you keep looking at me like that?" I asked, feeling a blush creep up my cheeks.

He smiled, reaching across the table to take my hand. "Because I'm happy you're here. And because I'm thinking about our future."

I squeezed his hand, the warmth of his touch grounding me. "I'm happy to be here too," I said softly.

After we picked up the food, Tobi drove me to his house. We pulled up to the compound. Tobi helped me with my bags and walked inside. It was so peaceful and quiet compared to Lagos.

"Make yourself at home," he said, placing my bags in the room. "I need to head back to work for a bit, but I'll be back soon."

I nodded, feeling a pang of disappointment. I knew he had to work, but that didn't stop me from wanting to hang out with him. "Okay. I'll be here."

He gave me one last hug, his arms wrapping around me tightly. "I'll see you later," he whispered, kissing the top of my head before heading out the door.

I sighed and wandered back into the living room, the silence feeling too loud in Tobi's absence. I decided to unpack my things to distract myself. While putting away my clothes, I noticed Tobi's work ID lying on the table. My brow furrowed. He always went to work with his ID. I picked it up and called him immediately.

"Your work ID is here, o," I said when he picked up. Which work are you going without it?"

There was a brief pause on the other end. "Ah, it's not a big deal," he replied. "It's Friday. I don't need it today."

That didn't sound like Tobi. He was always meticulous about his work stuff. But I hadn't been around for a bit, and maybe things had changed. "Toh, no wahala," I said, shrugging it off.

He chuckled. "Stop worrying about me and go get ready. According to the itinerary I sent you, I booked a spa treatment for you at 3 PM. You always complain about how stressful Lagos is, so I thought you could use some relaxation. I also booked a *Mani-Pedi* for you." Mani-Pedi is a slogan for manicure and pedicure.

I smiled, warmth spreading through me at his thoughtfulness. "You did all that? You're too much, Tobi."

"I just want you to relax and enjoy yourself. I'm sorry I won't be around to pick you up, but can you book a ride to go?"

"Of course," I replied, touched by his efforts. "You've already done so much. I don't mind booking a ride."

As the call ended. I decided to take a quick shower and change into something comfortable for the spa. By the time I was ready, it was almost 2:30 PM. I booked a ride and headed out, my heart light and mind buzzing with anticipation.

The spa was a sanctuary of peace. As soon as I walked in, the calming scent of lavender and eucalyptus enveloped me, and soft, soothing music played in the background. I was greeted by a friendly receptionist who confirmed my appointment and led me to the treatment room. The massage therapist was a gentle, professional Filipina woman who seemed to have magic hands. As she worked out the knots and tension in my muscles, I felt all the stress of Lagos's life melt away.

The massage was followed by a luxurious Mani-Pedi session. The nail technician was meticulous, and we chatted easily about everything from the latest fashion trends to our favourite movies. By the time she was done, my nails were perfectly polished, and I felt pampered and rejuvenated.

I checked my phone and saw that the spa session had taken longer than we anticipated. It was already past 5 PM, and I was running behind schedule. I quickly called Tobi.

"Hey, I'm done at the spa," I said. "But it took longer than expected. Can you come pick me up?"

"Of course," he replied. "I'll be there in fifteen minutes."

As I waited, I replayed the events of the day in my mind. Tobi's meticulous planning, the thoughtful spa appointment, and the way he looked at me with so much love and care. A thought crept into my mind, sending a thrill through me. Was this the night he would propose?

My hopes soared. I wanted to look my best. When Tobi arrived, he greeted me with that infectious smile of his, and we rushed home to get ready for the evening. I couldn't contain my excitement.

"I think I should get my makeup done professionally," I said as we hurriedly changed. "I want to look perfect tonight."

Tobi looked at me, his eyes filled with affection. "You're always perfect to me, but if that's what you want, go for it. I'll meet you at the venue."

I nodded, my heart fluttering with anticipation. "See you there."

As I made my way to the makeup artist, I could hardly sit still. The anticipation of what the night might hold was almost too much. The makeup artist, a skilled and friendly woman named Sade, noticed my excitement.

"Special night?" she asked with a knowing smile as she started working on my face.

"Maybe," I replied, unable to hide my grin. "I think he might propose tonight."

Sade's eyes sparkled with excitement. "Well, we better make sure you look absolutely stunning then."

She worked her magic, transforming me into a vision of elegance. By the time she was done, I barely recognised myself in the mirror. I looked like me, but the makeup accentuated my features. I looked extraordinarily beautiful and felt even more confident.

"Thank you so much, Sade," I said, hugging her. You're amazing."

"Go get your man," she replied with a wink.

I left the studio, my heart pounding with excitement and nerves. The ride to the venue felt like an eternity, and I couldn't stop fidgeting.

What if tonight really was the night? What if Tobi was finally going to propose? The thought filled me with a mixture of joy and anxiety. I wanted everything to be perfect. The butterflies that were always around whenever Tobi was concerned took flight in my tummy.

When I arrived at the venue, a fancy restaurant with an elegant, romantic ambience, I spotted Tobi waiting for me at the entrance. He had made a habit of arriving at every restaurant we had a date at before me. I thought it was chivalrous. And he had picked the same restaurant we had our first date at. He walked out to greet me and I smiled at him. He looked incredibly handsome in a crisp black shirt and blue trousers, his eyes lighting up when he saw me.

"You look stunning," he said.

"Thank you," I smiled up at him, enjoying the sweet scent of his cologne wafting in the air..

"You look amazing, too."

He took my hand in his and led me inside.

WHAT LOVE LEFT UNFINISHED

SURPRISE

*H*olding hands, Tobi and I walked hand in hand into the restaurant.

I couldn't lie to myself that I was a bit nervous. Tobi had gone above and beyond for me all day, but then again, he always did. I needed to manage my expectations and enjoy my time with him no matter the outcome. I took a deep breath and reminded myself that being with him was what mattered most. We were going to have a great time.

As we stepped inside, Tobi held his phone up, videoing me with that familiar mischievous grin. "Star girl, does this look familiar? Or maybe sound familiar?" he asked, his voice playful.

I laughed, immediately recognising the setting. It was just like our first official date—the same restaurant and romantic ambience. My heart fluttered as I remembered how special that night had been. "Tobi, you're unbelievable," I said, shaking my head with a smile.

He chuckled. "I thought it would be nice to recreate our first date. Bring back some good memories."

Tobi led me to our table, his eyes twinkling with excitement. "When I came in, I saw my colleague and one of my sister's friends," he mentioned casually, pointing toward a table across the room.

I looked over and saw two familiar faces. We walked over and said a polite hello. "Hi, it's nice to see you both here," I said, trying to mask my curiosity.

They smiled and exchanged pleasantries, but it seemed like just a coincidence. I wondered if Tobi had planned something more. Two familiar faces didn't seem like just a casual coincidence. My heart was racing. I looked around the restaurant and saw no other remotely familiar face.

I could almost see the restaurant filled with balloons, expect roses, and my friends and family present, and imagine Tobi getting down on one knee and asking me to marry him with everyone in my life screaming, "Say yes!"

But when we got to the restaurant and our table, there was no such thing happening. The restaurant seemed normal, with other patrons enjoying their meals, utterly unaware of the significance of this night for me. The breath I had been holding fizzled out in disappointment.

I noticed that Tobi had already placed our order. He knew all my favourite foods and drinks, so I more than trusted him to make the order for me. "You really thought of everything, didn't you?"

He grinned. "I wanted tonight to be special."

The waiter brought out our drinks, and I took a sip, trying to calm my racing heart. Tobi reached across the table and took my hand, his thumb gently rubbing the back of it. "Are you okay?" he asked, his eyes filled with concern.

I nodded, managing a smile. "Just a little overwhelmed, I guess. This place brings back so many memories."

He squeezed my hand. "I hope they're good ones."

"They are," I replied softly. "Very good ones."

As we waited for our food, we reminisced about our first date. The way we had both been so nervous, the awkward yet endearing moments that had made the night unforgettable. It felt like no time had passed at all, and yet, we had grown so much closer since then. Tobi's eyes sparkled as he laughed, and I felt a warm glow in my chest. This was the man I cared for, the man who knew me inside out, who always went above and beyond for me. I needed to manage my expectations, though. Tonight might just be another beautiful night together, and that was perfect.

As we settled into our conversation, I tried to reduce my expectations. Just then, Tobi's sister's friend walked over to our table, his face lit up with a bright smile.

"You two look so good together," he gushed. "Would you mind if I took a photo of you both?"

I laughed, feeling a little shy. "I hope it's free, shaa, because this wasn't included in our expenses. We budget all our dates and the picture would be no exception."

He waved a hand dismissively. "Of course, it's free! It would be my pleasure."

Tobi chuckled and wrapped an arm around my shoulders, pulling me closer. "Alright then, let's do it."

We posed for the photo, our faces close together, smiling broadly. The camera clicked, capturing the moment. It felt surreal, but I reminded myself to keep my expectations in check. After all, Tobi always did thoughtful things like this for me. It didn't necessarily mean anything more.

As we settled back into our seats, the waiter brought out our food. The aroma was intoxicating, and I couldn't help but smile as I looked at the spread before us. Tobi had ordered all my favourites.

"You really know how to spoil me," I said, my voice filled with affection.

He grinned. "Only the best for you, star girl."

We dug into our meal, savouring each bite. The food was delicious, and the company even better. We chatted and laughed, reminiscing about old memories and creating new ones. Despite my efforts to manage my expectations, a small part of me wondered if tonight was the night.

Was Tobi going to propose?

After dinner, Tobi stood up and held out his hand. "Come on, let's go take some personal photos outside."

I took his hand, feeling a flutter of excitement in my stomach. As we stepped outside, the cool evening air wrapped around us. Tobi led me to a picturesque spot by a balcony, where the soft glow of the lights created a romantic atmosphere.

Just as we were about to take a selfie, Tobi's sister's friend appeared again. "Do you want me to take a few more photos of you two? The lighting here is perfect."

I laughed, feeling a bit embarrassed but also flattered. "Sure, why not?"

He snapped a few more pictures, capturing our candid moments. When he showed me the photos, I gasped. "Tobi, look at these! They're beautiful. You have to take his number."

Tobi smiled and exchanged numbers with him, thanking him for the lovely photos. He waved goodbye and left us alone by the balcony outside.

I watched him walk away, a sense of finality settling in. That was it. The photographer was gone, and there was no engagement happening tonight. I felt a pang of disappointment, but I quickly shrugged it off. Tobi had put so much effort into making this evening special, and I was determined to enjoy it.

We enjoyed the rest of our meal, savouring the flavours. It didn't matter if it was good food or bad, I was having a great time. The food was delicious though, and the conversation flowed easily. Tobi's laughter was infectious, and despite the slight ache in my heart, I found myself genuinely happy. This was what mattered – the time we spent together, the memories we made.

As we finished our dessert, Tobi leaned back in his chair, a content smile on his face. "Are you full?"

I shook my head, feeling a mischievous grin spread across my lips. "Not quite. I could really go for some chocolate chip cookies from H-Medix."

Tobi laughed, shaking his head. "You and your sweet tooth. Alright, we can stop there on the way."

He hesitated for a moment, then added, "Actually, a member of my flag football team is having a party at a hotel nearby. Do you mind if we stop by for a bit? We just need to show our faces."

I sighed, feeling a wave of exhaustion wash over me. "Tobi, I'm really tired. Do we have to?"

He reached across the table and took my hand, his eyes pleading. "We won't be long. Just a quick hello."

Grumbling, I rolled my eyes. "Who does a party in a hotel, anyway?"

He chuckled and stood up, pulling me to my feet. "Come on, let's go."

We made our way to the car, the night air cool against my skin. As we drove to the hotel, I leaned back in my seat, trying to muster some energy. Tobi kept glancing over at me, a soft smile playing on his lips.

When we arrived at the hotel, I turned to him, suddenly feeling exhausted. "If it's going to be a quick hello, why don't you just go in and say hello while I wait in the car, especially since you said it won't take long?"

Tobi hesitated, then nodded. "Toh. If you want to stay in the car, I'll stay with you."

I laughed, shaking my head. "There's no need for us to have come all the way here just for both of us to sit in the car. We can't just both sit in the car. I'll go with you, it's fine."

He smiled, relief evident on his face. "Thank you. It really won't take long."

As we entered the lobby, I immediately noticed the odd silence. There was no music, no noise, nothing that indicated a party was happening. It was eerily quiet, the kind of silence that makes you hyper-aware of every little sound. The click of our shoes against the marble floor echoed softly as we walked.

I looked around, puzzled. "Where's the party? It's so quiet here. Maybe they're throwing it in one of the rooms and the hotel just has great soundproofing?"

Tobi glanced at me, a small smile playing on his lips. "Maybe. I'm not sure which room it's in. Let me call up and find out."

He pulled out his phone and dialled a number, holding it to his ear. I watched him, feeling a mix of curiosity and unease. Why was it so quiet? Shouldn't there be at least some noise filtering through? Maybe they were in a private suite?

"Hey, we're here. What's the room number again?" Tobi asked over the phone. He nodded, listening, then glanced at me with that same enigmatic smile. "Alright, thanks. We'll be right up."

He hung up and turned to me, his eyes twinkling with excitement. "Found it. Let's go."

As we made our way to the elevator, I tried to shake off my unease. This was supposed to be a quick hello, just a brief stop to show face. I could manage that. Tobi had gone to great lengths to make this evening special for me, and I wanted to enjoy it, no matter how tired I felt.

The elevator doors slid open with a soft ding, and we stepped inside. Tobi pressed the button for the fifth floor, and the doors closed, enveloping us in a cocoon of silence. I glanced at him, and he gave me another reassuring smile.

"Are you sure this is the right place?" I asked, trying to keep my tone light. "It's so quiet."

He chuckled. "I'm sure. Maybe they're just getting started. Or maybe everyone's inside the room. You know how these things go."

I nodded, feeling a bit more at ease. "Yeah, you're right."

The elevator stopped, and the doors slid open again, revealing a long, carpeted hallway. We stepped out, and Tobi led the way, his hand firmly holding mine. As we walked, I couldn't help but notice how deserted the hallway was. No signs of life, no sounds of laughter or music. Just the soft hum of the elevator doors closing behind us.

"Here we are," Tobi said, stopping before a door. He looked back at me, his eyes full of warmth and reassurance. "Ready?"

I took a deep breath and nodded. "Ready."

He squeezed my hand gently, then reached for the doorknob. As he pulled the door open, I felt a surge of anticipation. Maybe this was the big surprise he had been planning all along. I decided then and there that I would have a good time on his behalf, no matter what.

The door swung open, and we stepped inside. Even from the door, I could see that the lights were off.

FROM FRIENDSHIP TO FOREVER

....

Closer than ever...

A s Tobi pulled the door open, the interior of the room was enveloped in darkness, only illuminated by the soft glow of candlelight placed in heart-shaped cutouts on the floor. The gentle flicker of the flames cast dancing shadows on the walls, creating a magical, almost otherworldly atmosphere. I stepped inside, my heart pounding with excitement, and immediately let out a scream of joy.

The lights came on, revealing a scene straight out of a fairy tale. Confetti and rose petals were scattered across the floor, adding a whimsical touch to the room. At the centre, rose petals were arranged in the shape of a heart, with our initials, T and E, elegantly crafted within. Balloons floated around the room, some hovering near the ceiling, others gently bobbing at eye level.

On the side table, a white balloon with "Will you marry me?" written on it caught my eye. The 'o' in "you" was heart-shaped, making the message even more endearing. Also on the side table was a red pillow that said, "I'm yours, no refunds." Along with it was a bottle of wine, a teddy bear, and a Plushie.

I was overwhelmed with joy, my heart swelling with an indescribable happiness. Tobi just stood back, watching me with a loving smile, allowing me to soak in the scene. I took a few tentative steps into the room, feeling a giddy rush of emotions. The cool air of the room brushed against my skin, a refreshing contrast to the warmth of my exhilaration. The white sheets on the bed looked inviting, crisp and pristine, adding to the room's romantic ambience. I screamed in pure joy. My heart was so full.

"You lied to me!" I screamed in pure joy. I held my chest as my heart was threatening to burst out.

I walked further into the room, needing to steady myself. I reached out and held onto the TV console, trying to catch my breath. The giddiness was almost too much to handle, my legs feeling weak from the sheer joy coursing through me. I finally found a seat on the bed, sinking into the plush comfort of the mattress. I turned to my right and saw my friends, Jojo, Leke, and a few others, smiling at me. Their presence was the cherry on top of this perfect moment.

I screamed in joy again, this time falling to the floor, overcome with happiness. Tobi had gone above and beyond for me, creating a moment I would cherish forever. I hadn't even told my friends I was in town; I had planned to let them know once I had settled in. Yet, here they were, all part of this incredible surprise.

Tobi walked over to me, his smile warm and full of love. He helped me up and led me to sit on a chair in the room. Then, to my surprise, he pulled out a guitar. The sight of him with the instrument made my heart flutter even more. He strummed a few chords, the sound resonating beautifully in the quiet room. It was such a beautiful surprise. When Tobi and I first met, I saw a guitar in his room, just leaning against the wall casually. Over the time we had spent together, I kept seeing the guitar, but I had never seen him play it. I teased him about it often.

"This your guitar, ehn! Maybe one day, shaa, you will play it for me. Abi, you cannot play it?" I asked him often.

He would only laugh it off but never played it for me. Now, he sat looking deep into my eyes as he strummed the first chords. The soft and sweet melody enveloped the room in a warm embrace.

He began to sing a song he had made up himself while I sat on the chair to the side, smiling and happy. The lyrics were a heartfelt confession of love; each word was carefully chosen to convey the depth of his feelings for me. His voice was tender and filled with emotion, and I could feel my heart swell with

WHAT LOVE LEFT UNFINISHED

love and gratitude. Our future spread out before me, a long and beautiful life together.

I could feel my heart melt at the scene before my eyes as he sang, telling me to hold on. The song was a beautiful representation of our journey together, the ups and downs, the laughter and tears. It reminded me of how far we had come and how much further we had to go. I felt an overwhelming sense of connection, a deep bond beyond words, as he sang.

He then transitioned into a version of Jason Mraz's "I'm Yours," our friends chimed in, adding their voices to the chorus. Their harmony was imperfect, but it filled the room with so much love and joy. The familiar tune brought back memories of our shared moments, the nights we spent talking, dreaming, and planning our future together.

When my heart expanded to the point where I couldn't take it anymore, Tobi set the guitar aside. I could see the hard glint of determination in his eyes, the love that radiated from him. He took the balloon with "Will you marry me?" written on it; at the bottom, it was connected to a red ring box. He pulled it close to his chest, opened the box, and pulled out the ring. The sight of the ring sparkling under the soft candlelight made my breath catch in my throat.

He stretched the hand containing the ring towards me, and I felt a rush of emotions. My heart was pounding with excitement, joy, and disbelief. I was grinning from ear to ear, my face aching from the sheer happiness that consumed me. This was the moment I had dreamed of, the culmination of our love and commitment to each other.

He grasped it warmly and lovingly when I stretched my hand to him. His touch was gentle and firm at the same time. He looked into my eyes, and it felt like time stood still at that moment. Everything around us faded away, leaving just the two of us connected by an unbreakable bond.

"We die here," he said softly, his voice filled with emotion as he slid the ring onto my finger. It made me laugh in pure joy.

As the ring settled onto my finger, I felt a sense of completeness, as if a missing piece of my heart had finally fallen into place. The ring was beautiful.

I looked around the room, taking in the scene once more. The candlelight flickered softly, casting a warm glow over everything. The rose petals and confetti on the floor, the balloons floating gently in the air, and the smiles on my friends' faces all contributed to the magic of the moment.

Our friends cheered and clapped, their faces beaming with happiness. They rushed over, enveloping us in hugs and congratulations. Their presence made the moment even more special, adding to the joy and love that filled the room. I could feel their genuine happiness for us, which made my heart swell with gratitude.

Then, a soft melody began to play as if orchestrated by the stars. Tobi took my hand and led me to the centre of the room. My heart raced excitedly, and I could feel his warmth radiating through his fingers. He pulled me close, and I rested my head on his chest, listening to the steady rhythm of his heartbeat. It was a sound that had become my anchor, a reminder of his constant presence in my life.

We swayed gently to the music, our movements slow and deliberate. The world outside ceased to exist; it was just Tobi and me, wrapped in the cocoon of our love. I closed my eyes, savouring the moment, feeling utterly safe and sound in his arms. Each step we took together was a testament to our journey, a dance of love that had brought us to this perfect moment.

The room, with its flickering candles and scattered rose petals, felt like a dream. Our friends stood around us, capturing every moment with their cameras, their smiles reflecting the happiness that filled the room. The soft click of shutters became the soundtrack to our dance, a chorus of joy and celebration.

I looked up at Tobi, his eyes shining with love and pride. "I can't believe this is real," I whispered, my voice trembling with emotion.

He smiled, his gaze never leaving mine. "Believe it, Esther. This is our reality now. You and me, forever."

Tears welled up in my eyes but were tears of pure happiness. I leaned in, brushing my lips against his, feeling the warmth and love that radiated from him.

After our dance, we joined our friends for a series of pictures. Each snapshot was a freeze-frame of our joy, capturing the love overflowing in the room. We laughed and posed, the happiness infectious, spreading to every corner of the space. My friends took turns hugging us, their words of congratulations and well wishes echoing in my ears.

Jojo, with her infectious laugh, pulled me aside for a moment. "Girl, you look so happy! This is the best engagement I've ever witnessed."

I beamed at her, my heart full. "It's everything I ever wanted, Jojo. I can't believe Tobi went through all this trouble."

Leke joined us, his grin wide. "Esther, you deserve it. You two are perfect for each other."

I hugged them both tightly, feeling the love and support from my friends envelop me. Their presence made the evening even more magical, adding layers of joy to the already perfect night.

We continued taking pictures, each one a memory etched in time. There were silly poses, heartfelt hugs, and candid moments that captured the essence of our celebration. The joy was palpable, a living, breathing entity that filled the room and connected us all.

As the music played, Tobi and I danced some more, our friends cheering us on. Every step and turn felt like a dance toward our future, bright and filled with love. I was already overwhelmed with joy, but then Tobi stopped and led me to the side of the room, where a beautifully wrapped gift box sat on a small table. I hadn't noticed it before, and the sight of it piqued my curiosity.

He handed the package to me with a smile. "This is for you, Esther."

I looked up at him, surprised. "Tobi, what's this?"

He gestured for me to open it, his eyes twinkling with anticipation. "Just open it, and you'll see."

As I carefully opened the box, my heart swelled with emotion. Inside was a collection of items, each more thoughtful than the last. There was a castle made out of various currency notes. It was a hilarious yet incredibly touching gesture, especially considering the state of the country during the recent cash scarcity. During a particularly frustrating day, I joked with Tobi that I didn't have the old notes, the new notes, pounds, or dollars a few weeks ago. And now, they were all combined into a whimsical little castle.

"Tobi, I can't believe you did this," I said, my voice filled with awe.

He grinned, clearly pleased with my reaction. "I remember you saying you didn't have any of those currencies, so I thought I'd ensure you're covered."

I laughed, the sound bubbling up deep within me, full of love and amazement. I continued to dig through the package, pulling out the next item—a belt. I had casually mentioned to Tobi that I needed a new one, never expecting him to remember, let alone go out and buy it for me.

"Is this...?" I trailed off, looking up at him.

He nodded. "You said you needed a new belt, so I got it for you."

I shook my head, overwhelmed by his thoughtfulness. "You're incredible, Tobi."

There was more—a collection of my favourite candles and diffusers. Then, I found delicate gold anklets and waist beads. I had mentioned wanting to start wearing them almost in passing, not thinking much of it, but here they were.

He had thought of every little detail I had joked about or casually mentioned, and the intentionality behind each item moved me deeply.

"Tobi, you did all this... for me?" I whispered.

He nodded. "I wanted to make sure you had everything you needed, everything you wanted. You deserve all of it and more."

I was speechless, my heart so full it felt like it might burst. I loved how unconventional his gifts were and how much effort he had put into each one. This wasn't some store-bought gift basket; it was something he had curated himself with so much love and attention to detail. He paid attention to the details of all those conversations we had been having. There was something spectacular about being so seen, feeling so seen, that reinforced my decision to marry this man. I could get used to a lifetime of being this understood.

"And I even brought everything here, all your things, to the hotel," he added with a smile, "because I wanted this night to be perfect for you."

I looked around the room again at the scattered rose petals, the flickering candles, the soft glow that made everything feel warm and intimate. It was as if the entire world had narrowed to just this moment, the two of us.

Finally, as the night began to wind down, we stood together, taking in the scene around us. Our friends were still celebrating, their laughter echoing in the room. The candles flickered softly, casting a warm glow over everything. The rose petals on the floor were a beautiful reminder of Tobi's love and effort in making this evening special.

Tobi and I stood there, surrounded by our friends and the love that filled the room. There was laughter, music, and dancing, all set against the backdrop of the beautifully decorated room. As the night went on, I couldn't stop smiling. Whenever I looked at the ring on my finger, I was reminded of Tobi's love and our future together.

Eventually, the celebration began to wind down. Our friends started to leave, each offering their heartfelt congratulations again. The room grew quieter as they departed, leaving Tobi and me to soak in the moment. We sat together on the bed, holding hands and reflecting on the incredible evening we had just experienced.

"Tobi," I said softly, looking into his eyes, "this has been the most amazing night of my life. Thank you for everything. I love you so much."

He smiled, his eyes filled with love. "I love you too, Esther. I'm so glad you said yes."

We sat there in comfortable silence, enjoying the peace of the room. We smiled at each other, basking in the journey ahead. Tobi looked at me, happy and content. Then he spoke.

"This is a new journey we are about to embark on, Esther, and you know how crazy marriage can be—all the horror stories. We need to pray so God leads us. We might be good people individually, but this is uncharted territory. We need to commit this new phase to God's hands, " he whispered.

I smiled at him. It was exactly what I expected of him. That is how I knew I had picked the right man.

A LOVE DECLARED

The morning sunlight streamed softly through the hotel curtains.

*I*stirred, reluctant to leave the comfort of the bed, feeling the warmth of Tobi's arm draped protectively around me. It was one of those rare, blissful mornings when I woke up feeling that everything was right, and all the worries and noise of life were silenced by the overwhelming happiness that lingered from the night before.

Last night, I had been in a beautiful, enchanting dream I never wanted to wake up from. As I blinked my eyes open, I glanced over at Tobi, who was still sound asleep beside me, his face relaxed and peaceful. The corners of my lips turned up in a smile as I recalled every detail of the night before: the candles, the rose petals, the love and effort he had poured into making the proposal perfect. And he had succeeded. I couldn't have imagined a more wonderful, thoughtful way to begin our journey together. He had tailor-made every single detail for me.

I turned carefully in bed, not wanting to wake him just yet. Instead, I allowed myself the luxury of a few more moments of quiet reflection, simply soaking in the joy that filled every corner of my heart. I reached out and gently touched the engagement ring on my finger, which he had placed with such tenderness. The simple band was beautiful and understated but elegant. It wasn't flashy or extravagant, but it symbolised everything that Tobi and I had built together and everything we would create in the future.

The ring, however, wasn't the only thing on my mind. As I gazed at Tobi, still asleep beside me, I remembered what he had told me last night, just before we had drifted off to sleep. He had taken time off work—an entire leave—just to plan the engagement. That was why he hadn't been carrying his work ID with him. It made me smile even more, knowing he had gone to such lengths to make everything perfect. That was how much this had meant to him, how much **I** meant to him.

I felt so much love and gratitude swell in my chest. Tobi was always thoughtful and considerate, but…this was beyond anything I could have ever expected. He had gone above and beyond, not just in the proposal but in everything leading up to it. He had thought about every little detail, all to make sure that I would be happy. It was a feeling almost too big for words, making me want to hold him close and never let go.

As if sensing my thoughts, Tobi stirred beside me, his eyes slowly fluttering open. He blinked a few times, trying to remember where he was before his gaze settled on me. And then he smiled—a sleepy, contented smile that made my heart skip a beat.

"Good morning," he murmured, his voice husky with sleep.

"Good morning," I replied softly.

He wrapped his arms around me, pulling me closer. For a few moments, we just lay there, holding each other, basking in the warmth of the morning and the glow of our happiness.

"How are you feeling?" he asked.

"Happy," I said, my voice filled with emotion. "So incredibly happy."

Tobi smiled again, his eyes crinkling at the corners. "That's all I wanted."

We lay there for a while longer, just enjoying the quiet intimacy of the morning. But eventually, reality began to seep back in, and Tobi stretched, looking more awake now.

"I've got something planned for today," he said, his tone teasing.

I raised an eyebrow, curious. "Oh? What's that?"

Tobi grinned. "We're going shopping."

"Shopping?" I echoed, not entirely sure where he was going with this.

"For another ring," he explained, his eyes sparkling with mischief. "The one I gave you last night was just a placeholder."

I looked down at the ring on my finger, slightly puzzled. "A placeholder?"

Tobi nodded, his expression serious now. "My mom took me to this gold shop a while back. She advised that you should have a gold ring, one that you really like. But I didn't want to choose it for you. I thought it would be better if you picked out the ring yourself."

My heart melted at his words. It was so thoughtful of him, so typical of Tobi, to want me to have something I truly loved.

"You don't have to do that," I began, but Tobi cut me off with a gentle shake of his head.

"No, Esther. I want to. I want you to have the perfect ring you'll look at every day and know that it's a symbol of us and how much you mean to me."

I couldn't argue with that. The thought of picking out a ring together and having something truly ours filled me with an almost overwhelming warmth.

"Okay," I agreed, my voice soft. "Let's go pick out the perfect ring."

Tobi's smile widened, and he leaned in to kiss me again. "Let's do it."

The rest of the morning moved quickly in a haze of happiness and anticipation. We finally got out of bed, got ready, and headed to the gold shop Tobi's mother recommended. The city was awake and on the move, but I felt like I was floating above it all, wrapped in a bubble of joy that nothing could penetrate.

When we arrived at the shop, I was struck by its elegance and refinement. The displays were filled with beautiful, sparkling jewellery, each piece more exquisite than the last. I felt a little out of place as if I were stepping into a world that wasn't quite mine. But Tobi was right there beside me, his hand warm and reassuring in mine, and that was all I needed.

A friendly salesman greeted us and led us to a display case filled with gold rings. He opened the case and began showing us different styles, each more beautiful than the last. But when I saw the ring that made my heart skip a beat, I knew it immediately. It was a simple gold band, elegant and understated, but with a unique twist that made it stand out. A small diamond was embedded in the band, catching the light in a way that made it shimmer like the morning sun.

I gasped when I saw the price tag. It was expensive—more than I had ever thought about spending on a piece of jewelry. I turned to Tobi, my heart pounding.

"It's too expensive," I insisted. "We can find something else, something more affordable."

Tobi just looked at me, his expression calm and steady. "Do you like it?"

I nodded, unable to deny how much I loved the ring. It was everything I had imagined, and more.

"Then we're getting it," he said simply.

I stared at him, a mix of emotions swirling inside me. "But Tobi, it's…"

"If you love it, then that's all that matters," he interrupted, his voice firm but gentle. "This is your ring, Esther. The one you'll wear every day. I want it to be perfect for you."

I felt tears pricking at the corners of my eyes, overwhelmed by his thoughtfulness, generosity, and love. I had always known that Tobi was special, but moments like this made me realise just how deeply he cared for me and how much he was willing to do to make me happy.

"Thank you," I hoarsely whispered.

Tobi just smiled, that warm, reassuring smile that I loved so much. He paid for the ring without any second thought, and before I knew it, it was on my finger, sparkling in the sunlight that streamed through the shop windows.

We spent the rest of the day in a haze of happiness, floating from one moment to the next. We went back to the hotel to rest for a bit, the excitement of the past few days finally catching up with us. We lay in bed together, our hands intertwined, the ring on my finger a constant, beautiful reminder of everything that had happened, and everything that was still to come.

In the evening, Tobi told me that he wanted to take me to his family's house, just to share the news with them in person. I had met his parents before, on multiple occasions, but this time was different. We were going to them as an engaged couple this time, and the thought filled me with nervous excitement.

When we arrived at his family's house, his mother was beside herself with joy. She hugged me tightly, her eyes shining with happiness, and joked that she hadn't expected Tobi to get married anytime soon.

"I had even completely given up on him." She laughed.

"And here you are," she said, laughing, "getting married before thirty!

I laughed too, how could I not? I was caught up in the infectious joy that seemed to fill the entire house. Tobi's father was just as thrilled, clapping him on the back and welcoming me into the family with open arms. It was a warmth, a sense of belonging, that I hadn't realised I had been missing before Tobi.

Tobi was so proud, so happy, and he wanted to share that happiness with everyone around him. He took me around to meet the neighbours, showing me off like the treasure he believed I was. I could hardly believe it was all real, that this was my life now. I kept wondering what I had done to deserve this much happiness. Surely, it was too much for just one person. But the smiles, the laughter, the genuine joy of everyone we met— made it real and tangible.

His mother gave me a gift, a beautifully wrapped package that I couldn't wait to open. The neighbours, too, were generous, offering us their congratulations and small tokens of goodwill. It was overwhelming but in the best possible way. I was just as excited as they were, caught up in the whirlwind of emotions that seemed to swirl around us.

By the time we left, my heart was so full that I felt like it might burst. Tobi and I spent the evening talking, laughing, and dreaming about the future. We were both exhausted, but a good kind of exhaustion that comes from a day well spent and shared happiness.

The next day, we had a celebratory lunch at Tobi's mom's favourite restaurant, *City View*. It is a cosy little place with the best Biryani rice I have ever tasted. We discussed our plans, the wedding, and our life together. Every word, every moment, was filled with a sense of anticipation and excitement for the future.

Later that day, as we made our way to the airport, I noticed that Tobi looked tired. Happy, yes, but exhausted. He had put so much effort into everything, ensuring I was pleased and that everything was perfect. He had given so much of himself, and I knew he needed to rest, relax, and take some time.

As we pulled up to the airport, I turned to him, my heart filled with gratitude.

"Thank you, Tobi," I said softly, my voice filled with all the love I felt for him. "Thank you for everything."

He smiled at me, his eyes warm and tender. "You don't have to thank me, Esther. I did it all because I love you."

I reached out and took his hand, holding it tightly as we sat in the car for a moment longer.

"Get some rest, okay?" I said, my voice gentle. "You've done so much, and I'm so grateful. But now it's time for you to care for yourself too."

He nodded, his smile growing softer. "I will."

With one last hug, I said goodbye, my heart full of love and happiness, and I began my journey back to Lagos. As the plane took off, I gazed happily at the ring on my finger.

I couldn't wait to start the rest of my life with Tobi, who had given me everything I had ever wanted and more. My heart was full, my future bright, and I knew beyond a shadow of a doubt that I had made the right choice.

PART TWO

WAR BETWEEN NOW AND THE FUTURE

....

Life has the greatest surprise.

When I returned to Lagos, still basking in the afterglow of Tobi's incredible proposal, I didn't expect the next surprise he had in store. The joy and excitement of our engagement were still fresh in my mind, like the scent of rose petals that had filled the hotel room where he asked me to marry him. My heart was still dancing to the rhythm of that night's happiness when he called me, his voice brimming with something new, something 1urgent.

"Esther," he said, a smile evident in his tone even before he continued. "We need to start planning the wedding. I'm thinking we get married in the first week of April."

I was sure I hadn't heard him correctly. I paused, letting his words hang in the air as if they needed time to settle. A month? To plan a wedding? I knew Tobi was full of surprises, but this was on another level. I waited for the punchline to come, but there was none. He was dead serious.

"Wait, are you serious? We only have a month to plan the wedding?" I finally asked in shock. "Don't you want to rest from all the proposal planning first?"

He chuckled, that deep, comforting sound that always made me feel like everything would be alright. "Do you have a problem with getting married immediately?" he countered, his voice playful yet earnest.

I thought about it for a second. Did I have a problem with it? The idea of being Tobi's wife, of starting our life together as soon as possible, was something I had dreamed of. I knew that if there was one thing Tobi was serious about, it was this. If he wanted to get married immediately, then who was I to argue? Especially when the idea thrilled me.

"No," I said, a small smile forming. "I don't have a problem with it."

"Well, that settles it then," he replied, his tone final, but I could hear the excitement in his voice. It was infectious.

As much as I loved the idea of an April wedding, I worried about the logistics. Planning a wedding in such a short time would be challenging, and I was concerned that the urgency was because of something more pressing—**Tobi's permanent residency**. It was coming through soon, and we needed to get married quickly to be in the pool together. I pushed the worries aside for now. We would handle it together.

I knew Tobi usually let me have my way with most decisions, and this was the first time he insisted on something so quickly. It made me realise just how important this was to him. If he wanted it, then I was more than happy to oblige. The only caveat was that we had to move the date to the last weekend in April. That would give us a little more time, and hopefully, it wouldn't feel too rushed.

I took a deep breath, letting the tension in my chest release. "Okay," I said, my voice steady. "But if we're going to do this, I have one condition."

Tobi waited for me to continue.

"We need to move the date to the last weekend in April," I said, feeling a bit of my confidence return. "If we're going to pull this off, I need a little more time to ensure everything is perfect."

Tobi considered this for a moment, then nodded. "Alright. The last weekend in April it is."

Relief washed over me. A few extra weeks weren't much, but it would give us some breathing room and more time to plan and prepare.

Can we pull this off? Could we plan a wedding in just a few weeks? And more importantly, would it be the wedding we both wanted, the one we had dreamed of?

Despite the doubts swirling in my mind, I knew I had to trust Tobi—and myself. We had to set things in motion if this was even remotely possible. First, I had to tell my mother.

I decided to break the news to my mother over the phone one evening. The connection cracked slightly, but her familiar voice was a comfort.

"Hello, Mom," I began, trying to calm my voice. "There's something important I need to tell you."

There was a pause on the other end, and then she asked, "What is it, Esther?"

I took a deep breath, feeling the weight of my words. "Tobi and I... we're getting married."

Silence fell between us, heavy with her shock. I could almost see her eyes widening in disbelief. "Married? So soon?"

"Yes," I replied, trying to sound as confident as possible. "In April."

I could hear the concern in her voice as she asked, "But why so quickly? What's the rush?"

I hesitated, knowing I had to be honest. "It's because of Canada, Mama. Tobi's permanent residency is coming through soon, and we need to be married to be in the pool together. We don't have much time."

There was a moment of contemplation on her end. "Esther, are you sure about this? Marriage is a big step, and rushing into it..."

"I'm sure, Mom," I interrupted gently. "I love Tobi and want to spend the rest of my life with him. We're ready."

I could feel her hesitation but also her willingness to support me. "If you want this, I'll support you."

I was relieved and smiled as I said, "Thank you, Mom."

We agreed that Tobi would visit her again, this time as my fiancé. I told her I'd be coming to Port Harcourt the following Saturday, too.

When the day arrived, I flew to Port Harcourt to meet with Mom and make plans for Tobi to come and officially state his intentions.

Tobi flew in from Abuja that morning, and I drove to the airport to pick him up. My heart raced with anticipation as I waited for him at the arrivals gate, my eyes scanning the crowd for his familiar face. When I finally spotted him, my face split into a smile.

He smiled when he saw me, his eyes lighting up with that warmth that always made my heart skip a beat. "Hey," he said, pulling me into a tight hug. "You okay?"

I nodded, feeling a little more at ease now that he was here. "Yeah, I'm just... nervous. I mean, I know you've spoken with her several times, but this is different."

Tobi chuckled, brushing a stray hair from my face. "Don't worry. Everything's going to be fine."

I wanted to believe him, but the knot in my stomach refused to loosen. Meeting my mother was a big deal. Visiting to discuss marrying me was different than just a casual meeting, and while I knew Tobi was wonderful, I couldn't shake the fear that something might go wrong. Now, my mother would assess him beyond the idea of "my friend."

When we arrived, my mother was waiting for us at the door, her expression unreadable. Tobi's uncle, who had accompanied him, stepped forward first, greeting her with the expected customary respect and politeness. They exchanged pleasantries, and I could see my mother's posture relax just a little.

Tobi was next. He stepped forward, introducing himself with a slight bow, his tone respectful and earnest. "Good afternoon,

Ma. It's nice to meet you finally."

My mother glanced at me, her expression softening just a fraction before she turned her attention back to Tobi. "Come inside," she said, her tone neutral but not unkind. "Let's talk."

I followed them into the living room, and as soon as they settled down, Tobi spoke, "Ma, I'm here to ask for your daughter's hand in marriage formally."

My heart pounded in my chest as the words hung in the air. This was the moment I had been both dreading and anticipating for so many reasons.

I slipped into my bedroom, too shy and nervous to participate in the discussion. I felt like a little girl again, hiding away while the adults spoke about things I didn't fully understand.

From my room, I could hear the low murmur of their voices, but I couldn't make out what they were saying. My heart raced as I tried to imagine the conversation and guess how my mother was reacting. I wanted to be there and part of it, but simultaneously, I was terrified of what she might say.

After what felt like an eternity, the conversation ended, and I heard the sound of chairs scraping against the floor as they all stood up. I took a deep breath, steeling myself before leaving the room.

When I came out, I saw my mother smiling—an actual smile, not just the polite expression she had worn earlier. Tobi looked relieved, and his uncle nodded approvingly.

"We've spoken," my mother said, her warm and surprisingly gentle tone. "And I think you'll make a fine husband for my daughter."

A wave of relief crashed over me, and I felt a smile spread across my face. "Thank you, Mom," I whispered.

With the formalities out of the way, my mother insisted on making a meal for us. She bustled into the kitchen, and I followed her, eager to help and distract myself from the nervous energy still lingering in my chest.

She decided to make Onunu, a traditional Rivers State meal consisting of boiled yam and plantain pounded together with palm oil, usually eaten with pepper soup. I knew Tobi had never tried it before. As we worked together in the kitchen, my mother's mood lightened, and we chatted about the wedding plans, the guest list, and the dress I had yet to choose. It felt like a typical day, like any other time we had spent together, and it was a relief to have that sense of normalcy after the nervous encounter.

When the Onunu was ready, we all sat down to eat. I watched Tobi take his first bite, curious to see his reaction.

His eyes widened slightly, and then a smile spread across his face. "This is amazing," he said, his voice filled with genuine appreciation. "Is this going to be served at the wedding?"

My mother chuckled, clearly pleased with his reaction. "If you like it, we can certainly make that happen."

I felt a warmth bloom in my chest as I watched them interact. It was like a small but significant victory, a sign that things were falling into place and that this crazy, whirlwind wedding might come together after all.

After lunch, we set out to check out a few potential venues for the wedding reception. My childhood friend, Chisom, had kindly agreed to scope out some options for us, and she had given me a list of viable halls to consider.

The first two places we visited were lovely but didn't feel right. Something was missing, some intangible quality I couldn't quite put my finger on.

But when we arrived at the Golden Tulip, I immediately knew we had found the right place.

The hall was beautiful, with high ceilings and elegant lighting that cast a warm, inviting glow over the space. The hotel rooms were equally impressive, with tasteful decor and all the necessary amenities. It was affordable, yes, but more importantly, it felt right.

As we walked through the hall, Tobi and I exchanged a look, and we knew.

"It's perfect," I whispered, my voice filled with awe.

Tobi nodded, his expression mirroring my own. "It really is."

We didn't waste any time. Right then and there, we paid for the hall and the rooms we would be taking. It felt like a weight had been lifted off my shoulders, knowing that we had found the right place and that one more piece of the puzzle had fallen into place.

Deep in my heart, things were coming together, and I knew everything would be alright.

We still had so much to do and plan, but for the first time in weeks, I felt like I could breathe. We were going to pull this off. We would have the wedding we both wanted, the one we had dreamed of.

THE COUNTDOWN

Last steps to forever...

Tobi and I agreed to have the traditional and white weddings on the same day. It made sense, considering his family would be travelling all the way from Abuja to Port Harcourt. The logistics were challenging, but we figured it was the most cost-effective way to handle everything. However, finding a licensed church to wed us became our first real hurdle. My mother's church had recently shut its doors.

"Do you think Chisom's church would agree?" Tobi worried.

"I'm not sure, but I can ask her," I offered, hoping for the best. Chisom was always resourceful, and I trusted her to come through.

When Chisom picked up her phone to call the church, I held my breath. Everything hinged on this one call. My heart raced as she spoke to the church secretary, her voice calm and composed, even though I knew she was as anxious as I was.

"Good afternoon, this is Chisom. I'm calling on behalf of a friend who wants to get married at the church on the last Saturday of April. I wanted to check if the date is available.

I watched her face closely, searching for any sign of disappointment or frustration. I couldn't hear the other end of the conversation, but I saw Chisom's expression shift slightly as she nodded, listening intently.

"Yes, I understand," she said, her tone careful. She glanced at me and gave me a small smile before continuing. "Alright, I'll let her know. Thank you, and God bless."

As she hung up the phone, I could feel the tension in the room thickening. "What did they say?" I asked, unable to mask the urgency in my voice.

"They said yes," Chisom began, and I felt relieved. But she continued, "The priest wants you to call them directly. There's another wedding scheduled for that day, so you'll need to have your ceremony by 9 AM."

I took a deep breath, processing the information. "9 AM... We can do that."

Chisom nodded, her smile returning. "You'll just need to call and confirm with them. They want to make sure everything is in order."

Without wasting a moment, I dialled the number she gave me, my fingers trembling slightly. The call connected, and after a brief introduction, I explained our situation. The church priest was kind and understanding, explaining that the morning slot was available while they were booked for the afternoon.

"We can accommodate your wedding at 9 AM," he said. "If that works for you, you and your fiancé should come in to finalise the details."

"Yes, 9 AM is perfect," I replied. "We'll come by to see the pastor as soon as possible."

After hanging up, I turned to Chisom, barely able to contain my excitement. "It's happening, Chisom! We have a church!"

She grinned widely, the kind of smile that could light up the darkest room. "I told you it would work out, Esther. You're getting married!"

Later, we visited the pastor and set everything in motion. We had our first counselling session, and Tobi and the priest got along like a house on fire. After that, we went around to visit the oldest members of my family just to officially announce our intention to marry and give them a heads-up on the dates we had picked out.

By evening, I walked Tobi to his hotel. The excitement between us was palpable. I couldn't stop smiling, and neither could he.

Everything was coming together, and the future felt bright and promising.

"I can't believe how smoothly things are coming together," Tobi said as we reached the hotel entrance. I knew he was just as relieved as I was.

"Neither can I," I replied, squeezing his hand. "It's like everything is finally falling into place."

We stood there for a moment, just enjoying each other's company. I didn't want to let go, but we both needed rest. Tomorrow, he would head back to Abuja, and I would return to Lagos to dive headfirst into the whirlwind of wedding planning. It was just starting, but I had high hopes we could pull this off.

"Get some rest," I told him, gently tugging his hand. "We've got a lot to do when you get back."

Tobi smiled and pulled me into a tight embrace. "I will. And you too, Esther. Don't overwork yourself, okay?"

I nodded, leaning into him a little longer before finally stepping back. "I'll try. But you know me; I can't help it."

He laughed softly, the sound soothing to my frazzled nerves. "I know. But we'll get through this together by the grace of God."

As I watched him walk into the hotel, I felt everything—excitement, anxiety, love, and a little bit of fear. But more than anything, I felt ready—ready to marry the man I loved.

***

The next day, Tobi and I went our separate ways—he to Abuja and me to Lagos. That didn't mean we were going to relax. We had to set a budget, finalise plans, and prepare for the wedding. And with only a few weeks left, every minute counted.

When I returned to Lagos, the actual day-to-day of wedding planning hit me like a freight train. There was so much to do and so little time. To make matters worse, our budget was limited. I tried my best to make it all work, but my mind was constantly buzzing with new ideas, and sometimes, I couldn't help myself.

"Tobi, what do you think about hiring a live band for the reception?" I asked one evening, excitement lacing my voice as I held my phone close to my ear.

There was a pause on the other end of the line, and I could picture him frowning slightly, weighing the practicality of my suggestion. "Babe, that sounds nice, but do we have the budget for a live band?" His tone was gentle but firm, reminding me of our conversations about finances.

I bit my lip, feeling the weight of reality settle over me. "I know... but it would make the reception so lively," I said, trying to sound optimistic. "It's our wedding, after all. I want it to feel special."

Tobi sighed, his voice softening with understanding. "I get it, Esther. But we've already stretched our finances thin with everything else. We've got to be practical about this. We can't afford to splurge on every idea."

I rubbed my temples, feeling a slight pang of disappointment. I knew he was right, but the pressure to make the day perfect made me cling to every possibility, no matter how impractical. "You're right," I admitted after a moment, my voice quieter. "But I just want everything to be perfect."

"It will be perfect," Tobi reassured me, his voice full of warmth. "We don't need a live band for that. We've already got so much planned. Let's focus on what we can afford and ensure everyone has a great time."

I sighed, a mix of relief and frustration swirling inside me. "Alright," I agreed, trying to push the idea of a live band out of my head. "But we're not cutting corners on the food, okay? I want everyone to leave full and happy."

Tobi chuckled softly on the other end of the line, the tension between us easing. "Of course. We're not cutting corners on the food. I want everyone to leave talking about how great it was."

But as the days went by, the pressure mounted. Every decision felt like it had the potential to make or break the wedding. The bills started piling up, and so did the stress. Tobi and I clashed more than once, our disagreements over the budget and the endless list of tasks threatening to overshadow the joy of our upcoming union.

But we always found our way back to each other. Every time the frustration reached a boiling point, we talked it out and prayed. Our nightly phone calls became a lifeline, a way to remind ourselves that we were in this together, no matter how hard it got.

"Esther, we're almost there," Tobi would say, his voice full of reassurance. "Just a little more, and we'll be married. We can get through this."

And I believed him. Even when everything seemed to be going wrong—when the tailor ruined my clothes or the pressure of wedding planning became too much to bear—I leaned on Tobi. He was my rock, my anchor in the storm.

As the wedding drew nearer, I threw myself into the planning with a single-minded determination. I had only one maid of honour—Chisom, of course—and I wanted to surround myself with friends and family on the big day. I bought lace for my five closest friends, wanting only them standing beside me, their love and support giving me the strength to get through the day.

Then came the list from my family—the traditional list of items that Tobi would need to provide as part of the bride's price. When I saw the list, my heart sank. It was long and expensive, and I knew Tobi wouldn't be happy about it.

"I'm not paying that much," Tobi said firmly when I showed him the list. His tone left no room for negotiation.

I know it's expensive," I said, trying to calm my voice. "I'll talk to my mother and tell her that you will not be paying that much."

"They have to reduce the items," he replied, his voice softer now. "Because this is ridiculous. It feels like they're trying to sell you."

My mother, who had been listening quietly, bristled at his words. "We're not selling our daughter," she said, her tone icy. "I will speak to the head of her father's family. I am sure we can all come to an agreement here. I'll do my best."

I was annoyed. This was my father's family, who had done absolutely nothing to contribute to my life or growth after my father's demise, but they wanted to benefit from a union they knew nothing about. Tobi was adamant about not paying as much, and I supported him. We simply weren't going to spend that much.

Before the situation could escalate, my brother stepped in. "Let me handle this," he said, his voice calm and authoritative. "We'll work something out that everyone can agree on."

I breathed a sigh of relief. The last thing I wanted was a conflict between Tobi and my family. We needed to be united, not divided, especially close to the wedding.

A week before the wedding, the pressure reached its peak. I was buying things at the last minute, rushing to Balogun Market to get shoes and bags, and trying to fix my clothes after the tailor had botched them. It felt like everything that could go wrong was going wrong. And on top of it all, our plans for Canada finally came through, forcing us to cancel our honeymoon to keep the funds for proof of funds. It was a devastating blow, and the stress of it all nearly broke me.

But I refused to let it. I leaned into my support system—my family, friends, and, most of all, Tobi and his family. His family was incredibly helpful, stepping in wherever they could to ease the burden. And though I was exhausted, I knew I wasn't alone.

The day before I left for Port Harcourt, my colleagues at work surprised me with a small celebration. They showered me with gifts and well wishes, their kindness bringing tears to my eyes. It was a touching reminder that I was loved and that I had people in my corner no matter how hard things got.

When I arrived at Port Harcourt, I went straight to try on my wedding dress. But as I slipped it on, my heart sank. The dress wouldn't pass my hips. I tugged and pulled, but it was no use. It simply didn't fit.

Panic set in as I realised I had no choice but to rent another dress—one that cost an extra 50,000 naira—money we didn't have to spare. I worried the new dress might not be appropriate for the church, but my sister reassured me it would be fine. Still, the uncertainty gnawed at me.

As the wedding day approached, Chisom told me they were planning a bridal shower for me. It was the last thing I wanted—a party when I had so much on my mind—but I knew I couldn't say no. So I went along with it, putting on a brave face as my friends gathered to celebrate.

The shower went far better than I thought. My friends and sister showered me with love and gifts, and those who couldn't make it joined us via Zoom. It was a touching moment; my friends chose to be there for me. We were all in the moment, sharing cupcakes, laughing, and having an incredible time.

Tobi arrived in Port Harcourt the night of the bridal shower, just as my friends gave their heartfelt speeches and showered me with love and gifts. The moment I saw him, a sense of calm washed over me, a calm I hadn't felt in weeks. We were so close to the day we had been dreaming of for so long.

I excused myself from the circle of my friends, laughter bubbling up as I announced, "Let me go and greet my husband o." They teased me, telling me to sit down and enjoy my bridal shower, insisting I had all the time in the world to see Tobi later. But I couldn't help myself—I laughed, playfully shooed them off, and escaped.

I found Tobi waiting upstairs, a smile spreading across his face as I ran into his arms. We hugged tightly, the warmth of his embrace reminding me why all the stress and challenges were worth it. I pulled back just enough to sneak him a cupcake, which he accepted with a chuckle.

"This is for being the best husband-to-be," I whispered, and he kissed my forehead in response.

The days leading up to the wedding were a whirlwind of last-minute changes and unexpected challenges. When I thought I had everything under control, I realised I would have to change my traditional wear at the last minute.

By Thursday, I was making my cornrows, my mind racing with all the tasks that needed to be completed. Once my hair was done, I met Tobi at the church, where we finalised details with the priest.

In the middle of our conversation, Tobi suddenly turned to the priest and asked, "Sir, do you think Esther's wedding dress will be appropriate based on church rules?"

I froze, my heart skipping a beat. We hadn't considered this. The priest looked thoughtful for a moment before asking, "Can I see a picture of the dress?"

I quickly pulled out my phone and showed him the photo. The priest took one look and shook his head, a concerned expression on his face. "Ha, this dress won't work," he said, his tone final.

It felt like the ground had been pulled out from under me. The wedding was just two days away, and now I had to find a new dress. I was heartbroken, fighting back tears as I nodded and thanked the priest for his honesty. Tobi squeezed my hand, trying to comfort me, but the weight of the situation pressed down on my chest like a heavy stone.

We had just two days left. *How was I supposed to find a dress in two days?*

TO HAVE AND TO HOLD

···

The dress won't work?

fter leaving the church, I was barely holding it together. The priest's words were reverberating through my chest like a hammer against glass: *The dress won't work.* I had felt the sting of tears threatening to break through, but I swallowed them down. I wouldn't cry, not now, not when there was still so much left to do.

"Tobi," I said quietly as we walked toward the car, "can we please get some food first? I just... I need a minute."

He nodded without hesitation. "Of course. Let's get something to eat."

I could tell he was worried about me. His eyes kept darting toward me. I climbed into the passenger seat and stared out the window as he started the car, the hum of the engine filling the silence between us. My mind was racing, thoughts bouncing around, but none settled long enough to solve the dress disaster we had just encountered.

When we drove out, Tobi tried to lighten the mood. "You know," he began, glancing at me with a small smile, "we don't even need the church wedding. We can just move to the traditional wedding; after all, that is the Koko. That's the one everyone is looking forward to."

I turned to him, disbelief written all over my face. "Tobi, are you serious right now? We've been planning this for months. We can't just skip the church wedding!"

He shrugged, trying to keep things light. "I mean, we could just skip to the traditional part. It's the one that really matters, right? Your family, my family, everyone will be there. The church is just... an extra layer of paperwork."

I stared at him for a moment, my frustration bubbling up to the surface. I knew he was trying to make me feel better, but the thought of cutting corners, of not following through with everything we had planned, made me feel even more unsettled. "I'm not having it, Tobi. We've come this far. We're doing the church wedding. End of story."

He raised his hands in mock surrender. "Alright, alright. We're doing the church wedding. No need to bite my head off."

I sighed and looked away, feeling guilty for snapping at him. He didn't deserve that. He was trying to help, and I was letting my emotions get the better of me.

We arrived at the café, and I ordered waffles, hoping some food might help settle my nerves. As I ate, I could feel the tension in my shoulders slowly easing, the warmth of the waffle and syrup providing some much-needed comfort. Tobi sat across from me, watching me with a quiet intensity that made me feel both loved and guilty at the same time.

"I'm sorry," I said, setting my fork down after a few moments. "I shouldn't have snapped at you."

He reached across the table and took my hand in his, squeezing it gently. "It's okay, Esther. I know you're under a lot of pressure right now. I just want to help."

I nodded, tears prickling at the corners of my eyes. "I know. And I appreciate it; I really do. I just... I had a feeling something like this might happen. I should have prepared better."

Tobi shook his head. "You've done an amazing job, Esther. Seriously. If this is the worst thing that happens, then we're still doing pretty well."

His words helped, but I still felt angry. I couldn't afford to wallow in self-pity, though. There was too much to do, too many things still left to figure out.

"I need to call the shop," I said, pulling out my phone. "Maybe they can suggest something… anything."

Tobi nodded as I dialled the number, my heart pounding. The shop assistant answered on the second ring, and I quickly explained the situation, trying to keep my voice steady.

"Hmm, we could add a jacket to the dress," she suggested after a moment's pause. "It would cover your shoulders and back, and it should be acceptable for the church."

I frowned, sceptical. A jacket? On top of my wedding dress? It wasn't exactly the look I had envisioned. But what choice did I have?

"Alright," I said finally, my voice heavy with resignation. "Let's do that."

After hanging up, I looked at Tobi, watching me carefully. "They're adding a jacket," I said, sounding more optimistic than I felt.

"That's great," he said, reassuringly smiling. "It'll work out, Esther. I know it will."

I wanted to believe him. I really did. But the nagging doubt in my mind wouldn't let me fully relax. We still had so much to do before the wedding, and time was running out.

"We need to figure out the seating arrangements next," I said, mentally ticking off the list in my head.

"Let's do it," Tobi replied, his voice full of the calm confidence I had come to rely on.

We spent the next few hours finalising the seating plan, ensuring everyone would be where they needed to be. It was tedious, but having Tobi by my side made it slightly more bearable. He was my rock, the person I could lean on when everything else felt like it was spiralling out of control.

Once that was sorted, we headed to see Tobi's grandma and his family. I could feel the tension in my shoulders ease as we pulled up to their hotel. Being around family always had a way of grounding me, reminding me of what really mattered.

Tobi's grandma greeted us with a warm smile, pulling me into a tight hug. "My dear, you look so stressed," she said, her voice full of concern. "You need to take care of yourself, eh? The wedding is just the beginning."

I smiled, feeling a wave of affection for her. "I will, Grandma. It's just... there's so much to do."

She patted my cheek gently. "Everything will be fine. You'll see. Now come, let's sit and talk for a while."

We spent the evening with Tobi's family, and I felt a sense of peace settle over me for the first time in days. They were so excited for the wedding, so full of joy and anticipation, that it was impossible not to get caught up in their enthusiasm.

The next day, Friday, was our introduction, where our families would meet for the first time. I was excited but also nervous. This was the first step in officially joining our two families, and I wanted everything to go perfectly.

That morning, I had my frontal done. Looking at myself in the mirror, I began feeling a bit more confident that we could pull this off. This was it. We were almost there.

The introduction ceremony was beautiful and everything I had hoped for. Tobi's family paid the bride price, and as I was handed over to his family, there was a moment of overwhelming emotion. This was real. I was officially part of their family now, and they were told to take care of me.

After the introduction, we headed to the church for rehearsals. Chisom was a lifesaver, ensuring everything we needed was brought to the hotel and organising things with a precision that I could only envy. I was exhausted, physically and emotionally drained from the day's events, but there was still so much left to do.

As the day ended, I collapsed onto the bed in the hotel room, every muscle in my body aching. Just as I was about to drift off to sleep, there was a knock on the door. I groaned, rolling over to see Tobi standing there with a soft smile.

"Hey," he said quietly, stepping into the room. "I thought we could pray together before you sleep."

His request was so simple, full of love and sincerity, that I felt my heart swell. "Of course," I whispered, sitting up and taking his hand.

We stood outside in the dimly lit corridor, the hum of the hotel quiet around us. Tobi reached for my hand, his grip firm and comforting. We had a moment to ourselves, away from the bustle and noise of the day, and he led us in prayer. His voice was steady and sure, each word filled with the strength and faith I loved so much about him. He took my hands in his, and we prayed together.

When the prayer was over, Tobi kissed my forehead and whispered, "I love you, Esther. I can't wait to marry you."

"I love you too, Tobi," I replied, my voice thick with emotion. "I'll see you tomorrow."

Tomorrow was the day. Our wedding day. The culmination of all our hopes, dreams, and hard work. And I was ready.

The morning of the wedding dawned bright and clear, a beautiful day.

I woke up early, the excitement and nerves making it impossible to sleep any longer. Today was the day.

I slipped into a robe, my hands trembling slightly as I tied the belt. Everything was ready—the dress was sorted, the seating plan was finalised, and all the little details we agonised over were in place. Now, all that was left was to get to the church on time.

I took a deep breath and sat in the makeup artist's chair, trying to steady my nerves. She smiled at me as she began to work. "You're right on time, Esther," she said warmly. There was no last-minute rush, just the way it should be. Most of my brides are never on time."

I smiled back, feeling a bit of the tension ease away. Soon, my maid of honour, Chisom, joined us, offering words of encouragement and keeping the mood light. When the makeup was done and my hair was perfectly styled, they both helped me into my dress, their hands steady and reassuring.

As I stood up, fully dressed, I caught a glimpse of myself in the mirror. I was ready. It was time.

Tobi and I took pictures and were on time at the church. For all of their talk of being on time, the church workers themselves were late. It was annoying to wait, but what choice did we have?

As we waited outside with our well-wishers, my mind started wandering. I thought about everything that had led us to this moment, all the challenges we had faced and all the love that had brought us together. I thought about Tobi, the man who had been by my side through it all, and I felt a love so strong it took my breath away.

The doors finally opened, and a church worker greeted us. Tobi walked in, and I waited outside for the music I would walk in with to start. The sound of the music filled the air a few minutes later, and all eyes turned to me. I scanned the crowd, looking for one person, and when I saw him standing at the altar, his eyes locked on mine, I felt a sense of calm. Tobi was smiling, his face full of love and happiness, and at that moment, all his nerves and doubts melted away.

But then, just as I was about to take my first step down the aisle, I realised something was wrong. My brother, who was supposed to walk me down the aisle, wasn't there. Panic started to bubble up inside me, but before I could fully spiral, I saw him rushing back into the church with a sheepish grin on his face.

"Sorry, sorry," he whispered as he took my arm. "I'm here now. Let's do this."

I let out a breath I hadn't realised I was holding and smiled. "Let's do this."

As we walked down the aisle, I focused on Tobi, the love in his eyes, and all the fear and anxiety disappeared. This was where I was meant to be, with him, at this moment. Everything else faded into the background.

When I reached the altar, Tobi took my hand, his grip warm and reassuring. We exchanged vows; each word we uttered was heavy with the meaning of the purest kind of love we had built together.

And then, it was over. The ceremony was done, and we were officially husband and wife. As we walked back down the aisle, hand in hand, I felt a sense of profound joy that was almost overwhelming.

At the reception, I changed into the outfit we had chosen just a few days before. It was a whirlwind of activity, people everywhere, music playing, and laughter filling the air. But through it all, Tobi was by my side, his presence a constant source of comfort.

The day flew by in a blur of colours and sounds, but one moment stood out more than any other—the fireworks. We had planned a beautiful display, but something went wrong, and one of the fireworks caught fire. There was a moment of panic, but it was quickly put out, and the celebration continued without a hitch.

I customised my Ipele with "Iyawo Tobi," which was embroidered and beaded for my final outfit. I love the Yorubaness in that tag, having spent time in Lagos and forming solid connections in the beautiful and lively city, to the extent of getting married to a Yoruba man.

When Tobi saw it, his eyes lit up with pride, and I could see that he was as happy as I was. Everyone started calling me "Iyawo Tobi." I smiled every time I heard it, and Tobi did, too.

The night ended with us dancing, surrounded by our families, friends, and the people who loved us. As we cut the cake, Tobi gave the vote of thanks, his voice filled with gratitude and joy.

And just like that, it was over. We were married. It had been a long, exhausting journey, but it was worth every moment. As we left the reception, Tobi took my hand and squeezed it, a smile playing on his lips.

"We did it, Esther," he said softly. "We're married."

I looked up at him, my heart full to bursting with love and happiness. "Yes, we did," I whispered back, my voice thick with emotion. "We're married."

And in that moment, everything was perfect.

WHAT LOVE LEFT UNFINISHED

PART THREE

TOBI

"Dear Esther,

I wake up each day with a thought that anchors me, a single, unyielding truth that fills me with purpose: I love you. It's not the kind of love people write songs about; those fleeting flurries of emotion burn out as quickly as they ignite. No, what I feel for you is deep, steady, and enduring, like a river flowing long before I even realised it.

Esther, I've got to say being with you has been nothing short of amazing. You know how sometimes you meet someone, and everything just falls into place? That's how it feels with you. I don't always express it as I should, but trust me, you're the centre of my world.

Remember when we first started talking? You had this lightness, this infectious joy. I was drawn to you. I get that same rush whenever I see your name on my phone. It's like, 'Yes! Esther is here, and everything's going to be okay.'

Esther, I want you to know how much you mean to me. You became my anchor, my peace. When we first met, I didn't know that you would become so important to me, but with every conversation, every laugh, and every shared moment, my feelings for you deepened in ways I never expected.

I remember our chats, how we could talk about anything and everything, from the mundane details of our days to the deeper things that mattered most. Those conversations were like lifelines for me, a way to connect with you on a level that I've never experienced with anyone else. I found myself looking forward to your messages, the way you'd light up my screen and, more importantly, my heart.

I still laugh when I think about our little banter over who had more shoes. You were so sure I was wrong, and I was just trying to win a bet. It's those small moments with you that make everything so much better. It's not about the grand gestures or the big plans; it's about the everyday things—like talking about our days, planning our next hangout, or just joking around.

I remember that time you made me juice. You said everyone who drinks it gets addicted. Well, I didn't tell you then, but I got hooked—not just on the juice but on everything about you—your kindness, thoughtfulness, and ability to make everything feel right. I don't think I'll ever get enough of that.

You've always had this incredible ability to make me feel seen, heard, and valued. It's in the way you listen to me, remember the little things that matter to me and the way you're always there, whether it's to share a joke or support me when things get tough. I've never had that kind of connection with anyone, and I cherish it more than I can say.

Esther, you mean the world to me. I don't know if I've told you that enough, but it's true. You've brought so much light and happiness into my life. I wake up every day looking forward to hearing your voice, sharing my day with you, and just being around you.

You've always made me feel like I can do anything, be anything. With you, I feel like the best version of myself. I don't have to pretend or put up a front. I can just be Tobi, and that's enough for you. That means everything to me.

Esther, you are so much more than just a partner to me. You're my best friend, my confidante, the one person I can turn to no matter what. I've always admired your strength, kindness, and how you carry yourself with grace and dignity. You're the most beautiful person I know, inside and out, and I'm so grateful to have you in my life.

Do you remember when we were planning our wedding? How everything seemed so chaotic, and yet, in the midst of all that noise, we found moments of peace together. In those moments, I realised just how deeply I love you. Watching you handle everything calmly and with composure, even when things weren't going as planned, made me fall for you even more.

I've always loved how we balance each other out. Where I'm more laid back, you're focused and driven. Where I'm a bit of a dreamer, you're practical and realistic. We make a perfect team, which I don't take for granted. You've taught me so much, not just about love but about life, about what it means to care for someone truly, and I am so much better for it.

I think about our future together, filling me with hope and excitement. I want to build a life with you, Esther. I want to be the man who stands by your side through life's ups and downs, the one you can count on no matter what. I want to share everything with you, from the big moments to the small, everyday things that make life so special. You've become an integral part of my life, and I can't imagine it without you.

You once asked me what love meant to me, and at the time, I wasn't sure how to put it into words. But now, after everything we've been through together, I know exactly what it means. Love, to me, is the way I feel about you. It's how you make me want to be a better man and inspire me to work hard and dream big. It's the way I smile whenever I think about you, the way my heart skips a beat every time I see your name on my phone. Love is how you've become my everything and how I know, without a doubt, that you're the one I want to spend the rest of my life with.

I love you, Esther, more than words can express. I love how you make me feel and bring out the best in me. I love how you look at me with those eyes that seem to see right through to my soul. I love the sound of your laugh; it lights up a room and makes everything seem brighter. I love how thoughtful and caring you are and how you always put others first, even when it is difficult.

There's something else I want you to know, something I've been thinking about a lot lately. You've always been there for me through everything, and I want to be there for you similarly. I want to support you in all your dreams and goals and be your biggest cheerleader, just as you've been mine. I want to make you as happy as you've made me, giving you all the love and care you deserve.

You've told me about your worries and challenges, and I want you to know that I'm here for you every step of the way. We're in this together, and there's nothing we can't handle as long as we have each other. We die here! Your strength inspires me, and I want to be the one who helps you carry the load when it gets too heavy. I want to be the one who makes you smile, even on the most challenging days.

When I think about the future, I see us building a home together, a place filled with love, laughter, and the warmth of family. I see us growing old together, still holding hands, stealing kisses, and finding joy in each other's company. I see us supporting each other through life's challenges, celebrating each other's victories, and finding comfort in each other's presence. I see us creating a life rich in love, filled with moments that make all the struggles worth it.

I want to thank you, Esther, for everything you've given me— your love, kindness, and support. You've brought so much joy into my life, and I am endlessly grateful for you. You've shown me what it means to love and be loved truly, which I will carry with me for the rest of my life.

So, here's to us, our love, and the future we're building together. I can't wait to see what life has in store for us, but I know that whatever it is, we'll face it together, hand in hand, just as we always have.

I love you, Esther, now and always. Thank you for being my everything.

Tobi."

NEW BEGINNINGS ARE NOT AS SCARY BEING TOGETHER

*T*he wedding had been everything I had ever dreamed of and more. I could still feel the energy from the ceremony, the warmth of Tobi's hand in mine, and the joy that radiated from everyone who had come to celebrate with us. As we made our way to the hotel room after the reception, I was still floating on a cloud of happiness.

The room was beautiful—soft lighting, rose petals scattered across the duvet, and a bottle of champagne chilling in a bucket by the nightstand. But even with all the romantic touches, I could only focus on Tobi.

He sat down beside me, taking my hands in his. "I can't believe it's finally over," he said softly, his eyes searching mine. "We're married, Esther. We actually did it."

I nodded, my heart swelling with emotion. "I know. It feels like a dream."

He leaned in, pressing a tender kiss to my forehead. "It's real, and I couldn't be happier."

We sat there for a few moments, holding each other, savouring the quiet after the whirlwind of the day. I felt safe in his arms like nothing in the world could touch us. This was our moment, and I wanted to hold onto it forever.

Eventually, we decided to change out of our wedding clothes. As much as I loved my dress, I was more than ready to slip into something more comfortable. When we finally dressed, Tobi suggested we go out for a bit. "What do you say we head over to *Boomplay*? We could hang out with some of our friends. Just to chill," he asked, a mischievous glint in his eyes. "Just to chill for a while, unwind after everything."

I hesitated for a moment, still feeling the pull of the bed, but the idea of spending more time with him, just the two of us, was too tempting to resist. "That sounds perfect," I agreed.

Boomplay was one of the buzzing places in Port Harcourt—a lively place with great music, good food, and an atmosphere that was both relaxed and buzzing with energy. It was exactly what we needed after the noisiness of the wedding day.

When we arrived, the place was already in full swing, with people dancing, laughing, and enjoying themselves. We found a cosy corner and ordered some drinks, settling in to enjoy the vibe. I leaned back in my seat, watching Tobi as he chatted with our friends. His face lit up with that easy smile I loved so much.

As the night went on, we danced, laughed, and talked about the wedding, reminiscing about all the little moments that had made the day so special. I felt a sense of freedom and joy I hadn't felt in a long time. We were married. We had done it, and now the world was ours to explore together.

We didn't stay out too late, knowing we had the rest of our lives to enjoy nights like this. When we returned to the hotel, we were both exhausted, but the kind of exhaustion came from a well-spent day. We fell into bed, holding each other close, and drifted off to sleep, the events of the day still playing out in my mind like a beautiful, technicolour dream.

***

The following day, we woke up to the sound of birds chirping outside the window. I stretched lazily, feeling a deep sense of contentment. Tobi was still asleep beside me, his arm draped over my waist. I took a moment just to watch him, marvelling at how peaceful he looked.

I wanted to stay in bed all day, just like this, but there was so much to do. We had gifts to organise, thank-you notes to write, and a honeymoon to plan. But for now, I was content to just lie there, savouring the quiet morning with the man I loved.

Eventually, Tobi stirred, blinking sleepily as he looked over at me. "Good morning, Mrs. Ayo," he murmured, his voice thick with sleep.

"Good morning," I replied, smiling at the sound of my new name. "How did you sleep?"

"Like a baby," he said, pulling me closer. "How about you?"

"Like a woman who just married the love of her life," I teased.

He chuckled, brushing a kiss against my forehead. "That's because you did."

We stayed in bed a little longer, discussing the wedding and how everything had gone so perfectly. It was amazing to think about how much love we had received from our friends and family. The number of gifts and credit alerts we had gotten was overwhelming, and we couldn't help but joke that we might have actually made a profit on the wedding.

"Can you believe all these alerts?" Tobi said, scrolling through his phone. "It's like everyone wanted to spoil us."

"I know, right?" I laughed, looking over at the pile of gifts in the corner of the room. "We might have to rent a truck to return everything to Abuja."

He grinned, nudging me playfully. "Maybe we should just send it all by road. We can take the essentials and let the rest catch up with us."

"That sounds like a plan," I agreed, already thinking about organising everything.

We spent the rest of the morning sorting through the gifts, making lists, and arranging for everything to be sent to Abuja and Lagos. It was a bit of a logistical challenge, but Tobi and I worked well together, and the wedding planning honed our teamwork.

Once everything was settled, we packed a suitcase for our honeymoon. We had decided to keep it simple—just the two of us exploring Abuja and its surroundings. We weren't planning on going far, just enjoying each other's company and celebrating the start of our new life together.

Our flight to Abuja was booked for that afternoon, and as we headed to the airport, I felt a flutter of excitement. The honeymoon was the perfect way to unwind after the wedding, and I was looking forward to spending some uninterrupted time with Tobi.

When we arrived in Abuja, the first thing we did was check into our hotel. Tobi had planned everything down to the last detail, and as we entered the room, I was once again struck by how thoughtful he was. The room was beautifully decorated, with flowers on the bedside table and a view overlooking the city. It was the perfect romantic getaway, and I couldn't wait to explore it with him.

We spent our honeymoon hotel hopping; each place was a new experience and adventure. Tobi had a way of making every moment feel special, and I found myself falling even more in love with him as the days went by. We tried different cuisines—Lebanese, Japanese, and even some dishes I had never heard of. Tobi was always willing to try something new, and his enthusiasm was infectious.

One afternoon, as we were lounging in our latest hotel room, I stumbled upon an incredibly luxurious hotel online. The pictures were stunning—lavish rooms, breathtaking views, and amenities that seemed like they belonged in a five-star resort.

"Look at this," I said, showing Tobi the website. "This place is amazing, but there's no way we could afford it."

He glanced at the screen, raising an eyebrow. "How much is it?"

I told him, expecting him to laugh it off, but instead, he nodded thoughtfully. "Why not? Let's book it."

I stared at him in disbelief. "Are you serious? Tobi, that's a lot of money."

He shrugged, a smile playing on his lips. "What's the point of a small wedding if we can't splurge on ourselves afterwards? Come on, Esther. Let's do it. We deserve it."

His words took me by surprise, but as I looked at him, I realised he was right. We had intentionally kept our wedding modest and intimate so we could invest in what mattered most to us. And if Tobi thought this experience was worth it, then who was I to argue?

"Alright," I agreed, feeling a surge of excitement. "Let's do it."

That night, we checked into the hotel, and it was every bit as luxurious as the pictures had promised. The staff treated us like royalty, and our suite was nothing short of breathtaking. As I sank into the plush bed, surrounded by the opulence of our surroundings, I felt incredibly grateful for the life we were building together.

But it wasn't just the luxury that made our honeymoon special. It was the moments we shared, the quiet conversations late at night, the way we laughed together over something silly, and the way Tobi looked at me—like I was the only woman in the world. I definitely felt like the only woman in the world.

One of the most memorable moments was Tobi's father's birthday. We decided to take his parents out to celebrate, choosing a quaint restaurant known for its cosy ambience and exquisite cuisine. The evening was filled with laughter and stories, and it was clear how much Tobi's parents adored him. They warmly welcomed me, making me feel like I had been part of the family all along.

I felt a deep sense of belonging as we toasted to his father's health and happiness. I was not just Tobi's wife; I was a part of his family, and they had embraced me fully. It was a feeling I would treasure forever.

The following Sunday, we attended the Thanksgiving service at Tobi's church. It was our way of giving thanks for the wedding and all the blessings we had received. The church was filled with familiar faces, all greeting us with warmth and congratulations.

After the service, we were surrounded by well-wishers. The church women fussed over me, calling me "Tobi's wife" with such pride that it made me blush. The youth group even came over to introduce themselves and tell me about their meeting days, letting me know I was now part of the fold.

It was a beautiful feeling to be welcomed so openly into Tobi's world. And it wasn't just the church members who made me feel at home. Tobi's mother had mentioned earlier that she wanted to have a conversation with me, and I made some time to talk with her before the Sunday I was to leave.

I found her at the house. Mrs. Ayo looked at me with those kind eyes, and I could see the love she had for her son reflected in them.

"Esther," she began, her voice soft but firm, "I wanted to talk to you about Tobi."

I nodded, my heart beating a little faster. I wasn't sure what to expect, but I knew whatever she said would be important.

She reached out and took my hand, her grip warm and reassuring. "You know, no one is perfect, not even my son. But I want you to love him for who he is, with all his strengths and weaknesses."

Her words were like a balm to my soul. I could see how much she cared for her son, and it mirrored the love I had for him. "I do love him, Mummy," I said softly. "I love him with all my heart."

She smiled, her eyes shining with emotion. "That's all I ask. Just love him and be patient with him. Marriage isn't always easy, but if you love each other and work together, you can get through anything."

I felt tears prick at the corners of my eyes. This woman, who had raised the man I loved, was now welcoming me into her heart as well. "Thank you," I whispered, my voice thick with emotion. Thank you for trusting me with your son."

She squeezed my hand, her smile widening. "You're not just my daughter-in-law; you're my daughter now. And I want you to know I'm always here for you."

Tears spilt over me as I leaned in to hug her, my heart swelling with gratitude. I was truly blessed to have Mrs. Ayo as my second mother. Tobi's parents were amazing—open, welcoming, and kind. There was nothing I couldn't talk to them about, and that brought me a sense of security I hadn't expected.

After the service, Tobi and I headed back to our place to rest a bit before going to his parent's place. The man with the oldest marriage in Tobi's church was already there, waiting to see us. As we made our way there, I teased Tobi.

"How do you know so many people?" I asked, nudging him playfully. "You can relate to anyone, regardless of age."

He chuckled, shaking his head. "It's a gift, I guess. We thank God."

When we arrived, the old man greeted us warmly and offered us some money and words of encouragement. I was moved.

Afterward, we went out to lunch with Tobi's family. It was a relaxed and enjoyable meal that perfectly capped off our time in Abuja. As we sat around the table, I realised that I was content.

This was what family was all about—being there for each other, celebrating the good times, and supporting each other through the challenges.

Later that afternoon, Tobi and I headed to the airport, ready to catch my flight back to Lagos. But as luck would have it, the runway was blocked, and I couldn't fly out that day. I sent my office photos of the blocked runway to explain my absence from the office because there was no way I would have made it.

On the one hand, I was ready to return to Lagos and return to our routine. But on the other hand, it felt like God was giving us a little more time to savour this moment, to hold on to the magic of our honeymoon just a bit longer.

I was determined to enjoy the extra time I was given, but I knew it would be a drop in the bucket compared to the lifetime we had to spend together. I took an Uber back in the rain, and Tobi, of course, was overjoyed that we would spend another day together.

WHAT LOVE LEFT UNFINISHED

THE BLISSFUL SHADOW OF DREAMS

....

It feels wrong to leave a part of your heart behind...

We had spent the past few weeks in a blissful haze, wrapped up in the excitement of our wedding and the joy of being together, and now it was time to return to reality. I was in the car with Tobi, heading to the airport.

I glanced at Tobi as he drove, his face calm but his eyes betraying the sadness he felt. He caught me looking and smiled, though it didn't quite reach his eyes. "Are you okay?" he asked softly, his hand reaching out to rest on my knee.

I nodded, not trusting myself to speak. The truth was, I wasn't okay. The thought of leaving him, of returning to Lagos alone, felt like a punch to the gut. But I knew this was necessary. Our lives were in different cities for now, and we had to make it work, no matter how much it hurt.

As we pulled into the airport parking lot, Tobi turned off the engine and sat back in his seat, staring straight ahead. "I'm going to miss you," he said so quietly that my chest tightened in response.

I reached out and took his hand, squeezing it gently. "I'm going to miss you too," I whispered, my voice barely audible over the lump in my throat.

Tobi turned to me, his eyes searching mine like he was trying to memorise every detail of my face. "I can't stand the thought of not seeing you for a long while, Esther. It feels wrong, like something's missing when you're not with me," he said, his voice filled with a raw intensity that made my heart ache. He paused, then added, "In fact, help me book a flight to Lagos. I want to come back in two days."

I swallowed hard, trying to keep the tears at bay. "Tobi...," I began, my voice shaky, "are you sure?"

He nodded, his grip on my hand tightening as if he feared I might slip away. "Yes, I'm sure. I can't go more than a couple of days without seeing you. It's too hard," he said.

I fumbled with my phone, my fingers trembling as I opened the flight booking app. Tobi's eyes were fixed on me, watching every move, his expression softening as he saw the tears brimming in my eyes.

"I'll do it now," I whispered, my thumb hovering over the screen. "We still have some time before we reach the airport."

He leaned in closer, his forehead resting against mine. "I mean it, Esther. I'll be in Lagos before you even have time to miss me."

I sniffled. "Okay," I managed to say, trying to steady my voice. "Just give me a minute."

I tapped on the app, searching for flights while Tobi kept his gaze on me. He was so close I could feel his breath on my skin, his presence comforting amidst the chaos of my emotions.

"Here," I said after a moment, showing him the screen. "There's a flight in two days."

He glanced at the phone, then nodded. "Perfect. Book it."

I did as he asked.

"It's done," I said softly, handing him back the phone.

Tobi smiled. "See? I told you. I'll be there before you even have time to miss me."

I smiled through the tears. "I already miss you," I whispered.

He chuckled, pulling me into a tight embrace.

I didn't hold back the smile that spread across my face. The thought of seeing him again so soon made the looming flight back to Lagos a little less daunting. "I love you," I said, the words slipping out before I could stop them.

"I love you too, Esther," he said softly, his voice so full of warmth. "So much."

But as much as I wanted to stay in that car with him, wrapped up in the safety of his presence, I knew I had to leave.

We walked hand in hand into the terminal. Tobi helped me check in my luggage, his movements slow and deliberate as if he were trying to savour every last moment we had together.

When it was finally time for me to go through security, I turned to him, my heart aching with the thought of saying goodbye. "I'll see you in two days, right?" I asked, needing reassurance.

He nodded, pulling me into a tight hug. "Two days," he promised, his voice muffled against my hair. "Just two days."

I held onto him for a moment longer, not wanting to let go. But eventually, I had to. With one last lingering look, I turned and walked through the gate, forcing myself not to look back.

As I settled into my seat on the plane, I couldn't stop smiling. The thought of Tobi flying to Lagos in two days made the separation bearable. It was like having a piece of him with me, even as the distance between us grew.

***

When I arrived in Lagos, the city was its usual chaotic self. The familiar sounds of honking cars, the distant hum of generators, and the chatter of people filled the air as I made my way to my brother's house in Yaba. Being back in the city without Tobi by my side felt strange, but knowing that I would see him soon kept my spirits up.

The next morning, I woke up early, ready to return to my routine and head to work. I got dressed and prepared for the day ahead. But as I grabbed my keys and headed to my car, I was met with an unexpected obstacle.

My car engine wouldn't start.

I tried again, but the car remained stubbornly silent. Frustration bubbled up inside me as I sat behind the wheel, staring at the dashboard. This was the last thing I needed, especially on my first day back.

Without thinking, I reached for my phone and called Tobi. He picked up almost immediately, his voice warm and reassuring. "Hey, babe," he greeted me. "What's up?"

"My car won't start," I said, trying to keep the frustration out of my voice.

There was a brief pause on the other end of the line before Tobi responded. "What are we going to do?"

His words surprise me. *We.* He had said *we,* not *you.* Despite the stressful situation, I couldn't help the smile that spread across my face. It was such a simple thing, but it meant the world to me. Tobi wasn't just offering to help—he was making my problem his own. For the first time in my life, I felt like someone was truly in this with me, like I wasn't facing life's challenges alone.

"We'll figure it out," I said, feeling a warmth in my chest that had nothing to do with the Lagos heat. "But thank you for being there for me."

"Always," Tobi replied, and I could hear the sincerity in his voice. "Just let me know if you need anything, okay? We'll get through this together."

Those words stayed with me as I made arrangements to get to work without my car. It wasn't an ideal start to the day, but knowing that Tobi was there for me, even from miles away, made it easier to handle.

Two days later, just as he had promised, Tobi arrived in Lagos. The moment I saw him, all the stress and anxiety of the past few days melted away. Just being in his presence made me feel lighter and happier.

But life, as it often does, threw us a curveball. On the second day of his visit, while I was at work, Tobi received an email from a company in Nigeria where he had applied for a job. He had been so hopeful, so confident that this would be the opportunity he had been waiting for.

When I checked my phone during a break, I saw a message from him. My heart sank as I read his words: *"Got the email. Rejected."*

I could picture the disappointment on his face, the way he would be sitting heavily on the couch, staring blankly at the screen.

I quickly called him, wanting to be there for him, even if only through the phone. "Tobi," I said softly when he answered, my voice filled with concern. "I just saw your message. I'm so sorry."

He didn't say much, just a quiet "Yeah."

I could hear the sadness in his voice, and it made my heart ache. "I know how much this meant to you," I continued, trying to find the right words. "This job... I know you were counting on it."

There was a pause, and then he finally spoke, his voice filled with a kind of resigned sadness that made me sadder. "I just... I really thought this was it, you know? The job that would have given us more financial leverage for Canada that would give us the future we've been planning."

"I know," I said, wishing I could be there with him, to hold him, to take away his pain. "But this rejection doesn't define you. It doesn't take away everything you've accomplished or the amazing person you are."

"I'm not so sure," he murmured, the sadness still heavy in his voice.

As I sat there in my office, feeling helpless, an idea came to me. It was simple, but maybe it could bring a little light into his day. "Listen. Just relax, okay?"

He didn't argue, just sighed and said, "Okay."

As soon as I hung up, I grabbed my phone and quickly placed an order with our favourite local pizza place, *Panarottis*. I added a note for the delivery driver to include with the pizza.

A short while later, I got a text from Tobi. *"Did you order pizza?"*

"Maybe," I replied, smiling at the thought of his confusion.

"There's a note," he texted back, and I could almost hear the curiosity in his voice.

The note was simple, just a few words to remind him that he was loved, that this rejection didn't define him, and that I was there for him no matter what. I waited anxiously for his reply, hoping it would lift his spirits.

A moment later, my phone buzzed with a new message: *"You always know how to make me feel better. Thank you, babe."*

As I sat there in my office, knowing I couldn't be with him in person, I felt a little better knowing that at least I could be there for him in this small way. No matter what challenges we faced, we would face them together. And there was always pizza.

Because that's what marriage was, I realised. It was about being there for each other, even when things didn't go as planned.

Tobi's mood remained low since the rejection from the job, and I knew I could do little to take away the sting. But I also knew how much he loved food, how a good meal could brighten his day even in the smallest way. So, I made it my mission to load him up with all his favourites. Shawarma tonight, Jollof Rice and plantain tomorrow, and Suya the day after. It was a way to show him that I cared, was in this with him, and would do whatever it took to make him feel better.

When I got home that evening, Tobi was sitting on the couch, his phone in his hand, but his eyes were distant. I could tell he was still lost in his thoughts, still processing the disappointment. As I walked in, his gaze shifted, and a small smile touched his lips when he saw the bag in my hand.

"More food?" he teased, trying to lighten the mood.

"Always," I replied, smiling back. "You need to keep your strength up, Mr. Ayo."

He chuckled, but his eyes were softened as he took the shawarma from me. "You're too good to me, Esther. By the time I leave, I'll be so fat, you'll have to roll me out of here. See, my cheeks are even getting fat," he said, his voice filled with genuine appreciation.

"I'm just doing what any wife would do," I shrugged, even though I knew it was more than that. It was love, pure and simple.

Over the next few days, this became our routine. I'd come home with something special for him, and we'd eat together, discussing anything and everything, even the job rejection. I wanted to give him space to feel what he was feeling, but I also wanted to remind him that life was still full of little joys—like a perfectly cooked meal or a shared laugh over dinner.

It got to the point where Tobi refused to eat until I got home. He'd wait, sometimes for hours, so that we could share our meals. It became a kind of ritual, a way to reconnect at the end of the day.

One evening, as I was frying plantains—because no meal in our house was complete without dodo—my sister and her husband came by. They watched me move around the kitchen, flipping the plantains with practiced ease.

"Look at Esther, busy frying plantain for her husband," my sister teased, her voice filled with playful affection. "You've turned into a proper wife, o!"

I laughed, shaking my head. "Abeg, leave me alone. If I don't fry it, who will?"

They both laughed, and I felt a warmth in my chest. It was nice to have them around and share these moments with those I loved.

After dinner, Tobi and I visited my sister's father-in-law. We wanted to say "thank you" for supporting us during the wedding, and it was a good excuse to leave the house for a bit.

After Tobi had returned to Abuja in the last week of May, he called me, and I could tell from his tone that he had something on his mind.

"You know," he began, his voice crackling slightly through the phone, "the basketball team, and some other folks are organising a party to celebrate our wedding."

"A party?" I repeated, surprised. "That's so sweet of them."

"Yeah," he said, nodding even though I couldn't see him. "They've set it for June 10th."

I did a quick mental calculation. June 10th wasn't far off, and we were supposed to be in Port Harcourt by the 16th for another event. That didn't leave us much time to breathe, let alone recover from all the flying back and forth.

"When you were in Lagos, we didn't even know about the party," I said, half to myself.

Tobi chuckled softly. "Yeah, it came up after I got back to Abuja. I guess they wanted to surprise us, but I thought I should let you know so we can plan accordingly."

"Can we not push it to July? It might be a tight schedule." I tried.

Tobi sighed slightly, considering my words. "I know it's tight, but the excitement might die if we push the party to July. All the ginger would have died. People might not be as eager to celebrate with us."

He had a point, but I still felt uneasy about the timing. "But that's a lot of flying in such a short period. What if we're too exhausted?"

Tobi sighed, leaning back in his seat. "I get what you're saying, but I think it'll be worth it. We can make it work, Esther. We've handled worse."

We went back and forth on the subject for a while, each of us trying to convince the other. But in the end, I agreed to the June 10th party. I knew how much it meant to him and didn't want to take that away.

"Alright," I said finally, giving in. "June 10th it is. But you owe me one."

Tobi grinned, reaching over to squeeze my hand. "Deal. I'll make it up to you by the grace of God. I'll book your flight for the 9th of June."

I sighed. "You know that is my father's remembrance. The anniversary of his death. It's not always a good day for me. But if I cannot fly on the 9th, I'll leave the morning of the 10th and still make it in time for the party." I offered. Tobi nodded in understanding.

"That's okay, my love. Don't worry, we will have a good time."

With that settled, we headed inside to visit my sister's father-in-law. The conversation was light and filled with laughter, a welcome distraction from the stress of the past few days. It felt good to be surrounded by family.

"This past week has felt like another honeymoon," he said, his voice filled with contentment.

I smiled, reaching out to brush a strand of hair from his forehead. "It has, hasn't it? Maybe we should make every week feel like a honeymoon."

He chuckled, pulling me close. "I'd like that. As long as we're together, every day is a honeymoon."

We fell asleep that night wrapped up in each other, the worries of the world fading away.

Tobi had to leave for Abuja the next morning, but only after booking my flight to join him on June 9th. I took solace that I would soon reunite with my beloved again. By September, the plan was that I would relocate to be with my beloved. I couldn't wait.

I looked forward to finally settling down with him in utter domestic bliss.

THE STAR FELL AND THE WORLD ENDED

*I*t was a quiet Sunday afternoon, the fourth of June, when Tobi called. I was in the kitchen, stirring a pot of coconut rice, enjoying the rich aroma that filled the room. Cooking had always been therapeutic for me, a way to unwind after a long week, and today was no different. The rice was nearly done, and I was just about to start plating when my phone buzzed on the counter.

I wiped my hands on a towel and picked it up, smiling when I saw Tobi's name flash on the screen. "Hey, you," I greeted him warmly. "What's up?"

There was a pause on the other end of the line, a moment of hesitation that made me wonder what he was about to say. "I'm cooking," he finally said, obviously feeling pleased with himself.

I blinked in surprise, momentarily caught off guard. "You're what?" I asked, a hint of amusement creeping into my tone.

"I'm cooking chicken stew," he repeated, and I could almost picture the determined look on his face. Tobi wasn't much of a cook—he preferred to leave that to me or order takeout—but something was endearing about the fact that he was trying, especially for me.

I couldn't help but laugh; the sound was light and full of affection. "Chicken stew? Who are you, and what have you done with my husband?"

He chuckled, the sound warming my heart. "I wanted to make something for you. Something you can enjoy when you come over."

"Tobi, that's so sweet," I said, touched by the gesture. "But you know you don't have to do that. I don't mind cooking when I get there."

"I know," he replied, his tone softening. "But I wanted to. I know you've been working hard, and I just wanted to do something nice for you."

My heart swelled with love for this man, who always thought of ways to make me happy, even in the smallest ways. "Well, I can't wait to try it," I said, smiling. "But just so you know, I'm almost done making coconut rice here."

"Perfect," he said, his voice lighter now. "I'll keep the stew for you. It's going to be our little celebration when you arrive."

I loved how he said "our" and made everything feel like a shared experience, even when we were miles apart. "I'm looking forward to it," I said, and I meant it.

We spent the rest of the day on the phone, chatting as I finished cooking and cleaned the kitchen. Tobi's voice was a constant presence in my ear, comforting as I moved through the motions of my day. He told me about his plans for the week, about how he wanted to take his fitness journey seriously and start going to the gym more regularly. He had mentioned it before, and I knew he was determined to follow through with it.

By the time we hung up, I was still smiling, my heart full from our conversation. Tobi might not be much of a cook, but the fact that he was willing to go out of his way to make something special for me meant more than I could put into words. These little moments, these small acts of love, made our relationship so special.

As the days passed, I started planning for Tobi's upcoming 30th birthday on June 15th. I wanted to make it special and show him how much he meant to me. He had been going through a tough time lately, especially with the job rejection weighing heavily on his mind, and I knew he needed something to lift his spirits.

By the following day, I decided to start my week by paying for a three-month gym membership for him. He had been talking about it for a while, and I knew it would mean a lot to him to have that taken care of. I also knew how much he hated cooking, so I arranged for a woman to supply meals for him for a month. It was one less thing for him to worry about, and I knew he would appreciate the thoughtfulness behind it.

But the most important part of my plan was something a little more personal. I reached out to all of Tobi's friends and asked them to write something nice about him—a strength, a quality they admired, something that made him special. I wanted to create a jar full of these notes, something he could pull from whenever he felt down or unsure of himself.

The job rejection had hit him harder than I had initially realised. Tobi was the kind of person who took rejection deeply to heart, who always felt like he wasn't enough when things didn't go as planned. It broke my heart to see him like that, to hear the sadness in his voice whenever we spoke about the future. I wanted to remind him that he was strong, loved, and more than enough, even when the world seemed to be telling him otherwise.

Our plans for June were already shaping up to be memorable. We had a dinner date scheduled, a spa day, and, of course, Tobi's birthday. He had even saved the viewing of our wedding photos for that month, wanting to relive those special moments together. And to top it all off, the native outfits I had sewn for him had just been delivered. I couldn't wait to surprise him with them.

That morning, I pulled into the filling station and stared at the fuel prices in disbelief. It was the first time I was filling up since the last fuel hike, and the numbers on the pump were skyrocketing faster than I'd ever seen. I groaned as I started the process, watching the digits climb higher and higher. By the time the tank was full, the total had far exceeded what I had budgeted.

I sighed as I sat back in the driver's seat, my hand hovering over my phone. I needed to tell Tobi, not just about the fuel but about everything that was weighing on my mind. He was always the one I turned to, who knew how to make sense of the things that overwhelmed me.

I dialled his number, and he picked up almost immediately. "Hey, love," he greeted me, his voice warm, though I could hear the underlying fatigue in it.

"Hey," I replied, trying to keep the frustration out of my voice. "I just filled up the car, and you won't believe how much it cost."

"Really?" There was a hint of concern in his voice now. "How much?"

I hesitated, not wanting to sound like I was complaining, but I couldn't help it. "It's ridiculous, Tobi. It's the first time I've had to fill up since the price hike, and it's so expensive. I mean, I knew it would be more, but this is insane."

There was a pause on the other end, and I could almost hear him thinking. "Don't worry about it, Esther," he said finally. "I'll send you some money to help subsidise the cost. You shouldn't have to bear that burden alone."

I blinked, taken aback by his offer. "Tobi, you don't have to do that. I can handle it."

"I know you can," he replied, his tone softening. "But I want to help. Let me do this for you."

I felt a lump form in my throat at his words; I couldn't believe how kind this man was. Even when he was going through so much himself, he was still thinking of me and wanting to make things easier. "Thank you," I whispered, my voice thick with gratitude. You're too good to me."

"Never," he said with a slight chuckle. "Just making sure my wife is taken care of."

His words wrapped around me like a warm blanket, comforting and reassuring. They reminded me of how thoughtful he was and how, even in the midst of his struggles, he never stopped being the man I loved.

We spent the entire day on the phone, me trying my best to comfort him over the job loss. I could hear the disappointment in his voice, the way he tried to mask it with casual conversation, but it was there, lingering just beneath the surface.

"Esther," he said at one point, his voice heavy with frustration. "I don't understand. I did everything right. I prepared; I gave it my all... and it still wasn't enough."

My heart ached for him. "Tobi, you are more than enough," I said, trying to inject as much conviction into my voice as possible. "This rejection doesn't define you. It doesn't take away from everything you've accomplished."

"But it feels like it does," he admitted, his voice raw and vulnerable. "It feels like no matter how hard I try, I'm always coming up short. Like I'm not good enough."

Hearing those words from him was like a punch to the gut. Tobi was one of the most capable, intelligent, and caring people I knew, but in moments like this, all he could see were his perceived failures.

"You are good enough, Tobi. More than enough," I insisted, my voice trembling with the force of my emotions. "This is just a setback, not a reflection of your identity. You have so much to offer, and I know the right opportunity will come."

He was quiet for a moment, and I could tell he was struggling to believe me, to internalise what I was saying. "I just… I don't know," he finally said, his voice barely above a whisper. "I'm tired, Esther. I'm tired of trying so hard and feeling like it's all for nothing."

My heart shattered at his words. I wanted to reach through the phone, to hold him, to take away all the pain and doubt that was weighing him down. "I'm here, Tobi. We're in this together, and we'll get through it. I believe in you, even when you don't believe in yourself."

There was a long pause on the other end, and he sighed deeply. "Thank you," he said softly. "I don't know what I'd do without you."

"You'll never have to find out," I replied, my voice thick with emotion. "I'm not going anywhere."

As the day wore on, we continued to talk, sometimes about the job, sometimes about other things, but the heaviness in his voice never fully lifted. It was like a shadow that clung to him; no matter what I said, I could not fully soothe it.

By the time I got home that evening, I was exhausted, both physically and emotionally. My allergies were acting up, making my head feel heavy and foggy, and all I wanted to do was crawl into bed and sleep. But I knew Tobi needed me, so I called him as soon as I walked through the door.

"Hey, babe," I greeted him, trying to keep the weariness out of my voice.

"Hey," he replied, but a heaviness in his tone immediately put me on edge.

"What's wrong?" I asked, sitting down on the edge of the bed.

He sighed, and I could hear the frustration in his voice. "I'm just... I'm still upset about the job. I can't stop thinking about it."

I felt a pang of sympathy for him. "I know it's hard, Tobi, but you have to remember that this doesn't define you. You're still the amazing, talented person you've always been. This is just a setback, not the end."

"I know," he said, but his tone was flat as if he didn't quite believe it.

I tried to keep the conversation light to remind him of all the good things we had planned for the month. But nothing seemed to lift his spirits. He was stuck in his head, replaying the rejection repeatedly.

As we spoke, I could hear him call a friend of his, someone who had also been rejected for the job. I stayed quiet, listening as they commiserated, sharing their frustrations and disappointments. Hearing the friend say the same things I had been telling Tobi all day was strange, but I was grateful that he had someone else to lean on.

I texted Tobi, telling him to listen to her and really hear what she was saying. He didn't respond, but I hoped that he was taking her words to heart. When I got in, I called him again, hoping he would have cheered up. If anything, he sounded worse.

"Did something happen again?" I asked, worried.

He was quiet for a moment, and then he sighed. "I'm still in a bad mood, that's all. I just want things to go according to plan, you know?"

I wanted to press him some more, to understand, to console him, but I could sense that he wasn't ready to talk about it, nor was he ready for my efforts to cheer him up.

"Do you want to talk about it?" I offered gently.

"Not really," he admitted. "I think I just need to step outside for a bit to clear my head."

I hesitated, glancing at the clock. It was late, and I didn't like the idea of him wandering outside in the dark, especially when he was already in a bad mood.

"Are you sure that's a good idea? It's pretty late."

"The earlier you let me go, the earlier I can come back to you," he said, trying to reassure me.

Still uncertain, I bit my lip but knew he needed the space. "Okay," I finally said, relenting. "But please, be careful."

"I will," he promised. "I'll be back soon."

We said our goodbyes, and I waited for him to call me back so we could pray together before bed. Twenty minutes passed, and there was still no word from him. I tried not to worry, trying to tell myself that he just needed more time, but the unease in my chest wouldn't go away.

Finally, I sent him a message, asking him to please pray for both of us when he returned. I ended it with, "I love you" and "Goodnight."

Then I lay down, staring up at the ceiling. All I could think about was Tobi, out there in the dark, carrying the heavy burden of his disappointment alone. I promised myself that by the next day, he would feel better. It was going to be okay in the end. I just knew it.

Sleep came slowly that night, and when it finally did, it was fitful and uneasy.

WHAT LOVE LEFT UNFINISHED

THE DAY AFTER FOREVER

....

...falling, falling into a dark, endless abyss...

I woke up, and the first thing I did was check my phone to see if Tobi had responded. If he was feeling any better. My heart sank. None of my messages to Tobi from the night before had been delivered. The little grey ticks stared back at me like a taunt. That was odd. He always had his phone on him. Maybe he was still asleep. Perhaps he had turned off his phone for the night, too exhausted and wanting to be alone. Even though I knew Tobi would never have slept without at least texting me back, I shrugged it off. Maybe the network was bad.

I shook off the unease creeping into my chest and told myself I would call him when I got to the office. It was probably a network issue. That happens sometimes, right? I forced myself out of bed, trying to ignore the growing knot in my stomach. I moved through the motions of getting ready, my mind distracted, my heart restless.

As I drove to work, my phone rang, jolting me from my thoughts. I glanced at the screen and saw Tobi's sister's name flashing. A sense of dread overcame me, but I quickly pushed it aside. I didn't like picking up calls while driving, but something told me to make an exception this time.

I hit the answer button and put the phone on speaker. "Hey, sis, good morning," I greeted, trying to sound cheerful.

"Morning, Esther," her voice was serious, unlike her usual upbeat tone. My heart skipped a beat.

"What's up? Is everything okay?" I asked, trying to keep my voice steady.

"Tobi... I've been trying to reach him," she said, her words rushed. "Can you call him and tell him to call Mom and Dad? I've been trying to get a hold of him all morning, and Mom didn't sound okay when I spoke to her."

My grip tightened on the steering wheel. "Why do I need to call Tobi to call them? I can just call Mom if she's who you're worried about."

She hesitated. "Okay, but please reach out to her and let me know."

I shrugged; it was an easy request to fulfil. "Okay, I'll call Mom. I'm sure everything is fine."

We hung up, and I immediately dialled Tobi's number. It didn't go through. I decided to call Tobi's mom directly. She picked up after a few rings, her voice warm and familiar. "Esther, my dear! How are you?"

"I'm fine, Mom. I just got a call from Temi. She said you sounded worried about something and never called her that early.

There was a pause, then a soft chuckle. "Oh, Temi worries too much. I'm fine, Esther. Just a little tired, that's all. Are you on your way to work already? Ah, ah, my daughter, isn't it too early?"

"Yes, I am. With the fuel scarcity and the hike in price, I try to leave early to beat the traffic," I replied.

"I see. Smart girl," she said, her tone affectionate. Then, she added softly, "I want you to know, no matter what, I love you very much, Esther. Never doubt that, okay? You are my daughter."

Her words sent a strange jolt through me, a feeling I couldn't quite place. "I love you too, Mom," I said, trying to ignore the sudden tightness in my chest. "Is everything okay?"

"Yes, everything is fine," she assured me. "I'll call you later, alright? Take care, my dear."

We hung up, and I continued my drive to the office, the unease growing with every passing minute. Something wasn't right. I could feel it in my bones. The way Tobi's sister had called, the strange tone in his mother's voice... but I pushed those thoughts aside.

Maybe she was just feeling emotional today. She always told me she loved me, and this was no different. I was overthinking it. Perhaps today, she was just feeling extra mushy. After all, she was an affectionate woman; it was one of the things I loved about her. I was probably just feeling out of place because I hadn't spoken to Tobi all morning.

I arrived at the office earlier than usual; the parking lot was still mostly empty. I parked my car and decided to rest briefly before heading inside. I checked my phone again, hoping to see a message from Tobi, but there was nothing. The grey ticks remained. I tried calling him again, but it went straight to voicemail again.

A wave of frustration and worry washed over me, but I told myself to breathe. I would see him soon. Everything would be okay. I just needed to focus on work and keep myself busy until then.

A few minutes before eight, I got out of the car and made my way into the office. I forced myself to smile and greet my colleagues, but my mind was elsewhere, my heart pounding with anxiety.

I had barely settled at my desk when my phone buzzed again. I glanced at the screen and saw my brother's name. I frowned, my heart skipping a beat. What was he doing calling me this early?

"Hello, bro?" I answered, trying to keep my voice steady.

"Baby sis," his voice was soft, almost too soft. "I'm outside your office."

"What? Why?" I asked, confusion and panic beginning to creep into my voice.

"I just... I need to give you something," he said, but I could hear the tremor in his voice, the way it shook with an emotion he was trying to hide.

A cold, heavy feeling settled in my stomach. My heart started to race, a thousand thoughts running through my mind. Something was wrong—something needed to be fixed. Tobi's messages had yet to be delivered. He was unreachable. His mother's strange call. His sister's concern. And now my brother is here at my office. It didn't make sense. None of it made sense.

I stood up abruptly, my chair scraping against the floor. My breath was coming in short, panicked bursts. "I'm coming down," I said, my voice barely above a whisper.

I didn't wait for his response. I rushed out of my office, my feet moving faster than my mind could keep up with. I was too impatient to wait for the elevator, so I took the stairs, my heart pounding in my chest, each step echoing like a drumbeat in my ears.

I reached the lobby and pushed through the doors, my eyes scanning the parking lot. I spotted my brother standing by his car, his hands in his pockets, his face pale. When he saw me, he rushed over, wrapping his arms around me in a tight hug.

"What's going on?" I demanded, trying to pull away. "Why are you hugging me so tightly? What happened?"

But he didn't let go. He held me even tighter, his grip almost crushing. I turned my head, my eyes searching for answers, and that's when I saw her—his wife, standing a few feet away, her face twisted with grief. Beside her was my brother-in-law, my sister's husband, his eyes red and swollen, tears streaming down his face.

"What are they doing here?" I asked, my voice rising in panic. "Why is everyone here?"

My brother said nothing. He just held me, his body shaking. I felt like I was suffocating. My mind was racing, pieces of a puzzle coming together in a way I didn't want to acknowledge.

"Where's Tobi?" I whispered, my voice breaking. "Where is he?"

My brother finally pulled back, his eyes filled with tears. "We... we lost him, Esther."

I stared at him, my mind refusing to process his words. "What happened?" I asked, my voice trembling. "How?"

"There was an accident last night while he was riding his power bike and unfortunately he didn't survive" he responded, his voice choked.

The world stopped. The ground fell out from under me. I felt like I was falling into a dark, endless abyss. "No," I whispered, shaking my head. "No, no, no. That's not true. That can't be true."

"I'm so sorry," my brother said, his voice choking with emotion. "He's gone."

I couldn't breathe. I couldn't think. All I could do was scream, a raw, guttural sound that tore from my throat. "I warned him!" I screamed, my voice breaking. "I told him not to go out! I told him!"

My legs gave out, and I collapsed to the ground, my body wracked with sobs. "No, God, please, no!" I begged, tears streaming down my face. "It hasn't even been 24 hours… Please, just let me go back in time… Let me stop him... let me…"

My brother and sister-in-law tried to lift me, tried to hold me up, but I was lost in my grief; my mind shattered into a million pieces. This couldn't be happening. This couldn't be real. Not Tobi. Not my Tobi.

They managed to get me into the car, and my brother returned to the office to collect my things. I was too lost in my sorrow to process anything, my mind a blur of pain and disbelief. How could this be happening? How could he be gone?

My boss came down to the car, his face sombre. "I'm so sorry, Esther," he said softly, his voice filled with sympathy.

I looked up at him, confusion and anger boiling in my chest. "Why are you saying sorry?" I demanded, my voice shaky and weak. "There's nothing wrong. Tobi is fine. He's fine."

He just looked at me, his eyes filled with pity. "Take all the time you need, Esther. We'll cover everything here."

I nodded, numb. My brother returned, and we drove away, the world outside a blur. I didn't know where we were going. I didn't care. All I could think about was Tobi. My Tobi. How could he be gone? How could he just be... gone?

"Esther, listen," my brother said, his voice forced calm, like he was holding back some horrible truth. You just need to come to Abuja. Tobi is in the ICU; that's all. He just... he just needs to see you, touch you. He'll be fine. He just needs you." He tried his best to persuade me to calm down.

I looked at him, my mind refusing to process his words. "He needs me?" I whispered, my voice thin and hollow. "He's in the ICU?"

"Yes, yes. Just the ICU," he repeated, almost like a mantra. "He'll be okay once he sees you, Esther. He just needs you. That's all."

But the way they looked at each other and moved around me was telling a different story. My sister was pacing, her face pale, her lips trembling. And then, I heard it.

"Pack some dark clothing," my brother whispered. "She will be needing a lot of dark clothing."

Dark clothing. Needing. My stomach dropped. My heart began to race. "Why would I need dark clothes?" I demanded, my voice rising, panic creeping into every syllable. "Why would I need dark clothes?"

They exchanged glances, a silent conversation I wasn't privy to. "It's just… It's nothing, Esther. Just a precaution."

"Precaution for what?" I screamed, my voice breaking. "What are you not telling me?"

They didn't answer. I grabbed my phone, my hands shaking so badly I could barely hold it. I dialled Tobi's number, my breath hitching with each ring. "Come on, come on," I whispered. "Pick up, Tobi. Please, pick up."

But his line was unreachable. I tried again and again. Each time, it was the same: unreachable.

"No," I whispered, shaking my head. "No, this isn't happening.

This is all a mistake—a big misunderstanding. Tobi is fine. He's fine."

My brother tried to take my hand, but I snatched it away, glaring at him through my tears. "You're lying," I spat. "You're all lying to me. Tobi is not in the ICU. He's fine. He's just... he's just busy. Or he lost his phone. He's fine."

"Please, just... just stay calm." I didn't care who spoke.

"Calm?" I shrieked. "You want me to stay calm? You're talking about dark clothes and want me to stay calm?"

They didn't respond. They kept moving, whispering to each other, and packing things I didn't understand. My head was spinning, my chest tight with a fear I couldn't name. This wasn't real. This couldn't be real.

The drive to the airport was a blur of motion and noise, but all I could hear was my heart pounding in my ears like a drum. Every time I tried to speak, my voice came out in a strangled sob, the words caught in my throat like shards of glass.

"Tobi is alive," I whispered to myself, repeatedly, a chant, a prayer, a desperate plea. "Tobi is alive. Tobi is alive. Tobi is alive."

But every mile we drove, every second that passed, it felt like he was slipping further and further away from me, like I was losing him all over again. I could feel myself unravelling, the threads of my sanity pulling apart one by one until I was screaming.

By the time we reached the airport, I was barely holding on. My body was shaking so violently that I could hardly stand. I stumbled out of the car, my legs like jelly, my heart hammering in my chest. "This is a nightmare," I muttered. "It's a nightmare. It has to be."

My brother grabbed my arm, trying to steady me, but I pushed him away. "Don't touch me!" I screamed. "Don't you dare touch me! Where is Tobi? Where is he?"

"Esther, please," he pleaded, his voice breaking. "We're going to him now. We'll be there soon. Just… just hold on a little longer."

I couldn't breathe. I couldn't think. All I could do was scream, a raw, guttural sound that ripped from my throat like an animal in pain. I felt hands on me, pulling me, pushing me, guiding me through the airport, but it was all a blur—a blur of faces and voices and pain.

The next thing I knew, I was on a plane, the engines roaring around me, the cabin closing in like a coffin. My head was spinning; my vision blurred with tears. "Tobi is alive," I whispered again, my voice a broken record. "He's alive. He's alive."

But deep down, in the darkest part of my heart, I knew. I knew something was wrong. Something was terribly, horribly wrong. And I was terrified. I was afraid of what I would find when we landed. I was scared of what they weren't telling me. Frightened by the silence on the other end of the line.

I pressed my face into my hands, the sobs wracking my body, the tears pouring down my cheeks like a river. "Please, God," I whispered. "Please, don't take him from me. Please, don't let this be real."

But as the plane took off, soaring into the sky, I felt a cold, hard truth settle in my chest. Tobi was gone—my Tobi was gone—and nothing would ever be the same again.

A WORLD WITHOUT MY LOVE

The other name of grief is hope.

s soon as we were on the tarmac, my brother was already on his feet, pulling our carry-on down from the overhead bin. I barely registered his movements. My hand shook as I reached for my phone again, dialling Tobi's number for what had to be the hundredth time. **Unreachable**.

The same mechanical, indifferent voice over and over. **Unreachable**.

"Where are we going?" I asked, finally finding my voice, though it sounded foreign, thin, and distant. "Shouldn't we be going to the hospital? If Tobi is in the ICU, we should go to the hospital."

My brother's silence was suffocating. I turned to him, my eyes searching his face for answers he couldn't or wouldn't give. Instead, he just put his arm around me, guiding me forward.

"We're going to Tobi's house first," he said, and his voice cracked. "We need to… just need to…"

"To what?!" I snapped, pulling away from him. "Why are we going to the house if he's in the hospital? Take me to him now! I need to see him! I need to—"

My words were cut off by the tears I was swallowing down, the panic that clawed its way up my throat. My brother didn't answer me. He just pulled me closer, his grip firm but trembling. I could see how his shoulders tensed, and his eyes darted around, avoiding mine.

"It's a lie," I muttered to myself as they bundled me into the car. "It's a lie. Tobi is alive. He's waiting for me. This is all a big misunderstanding."

The drive to Tobi's house was a blur. I was screaming, my voice echoing around the car, bouncing off the windows, off their silent, pitying faces. "Take me to him!" I begged. "Take me to the hospital! He's not dead! He's not dead! He's not—"

They kept driving. They kept their eyes forward. And I kept screaming. My mind refused to accept what my heart already knew. **Tobi was gone.** No. No, he wasn't. He couldn't be. Not

Tobi. Not my Tobi.

We pulled up in front of his house, and my heart sank. Cars were lining the driveway and the street, as far as my eyes could see. People were huddled in groups, their faces sombre, eyes red-rimmed.

My stomach dropped.

"What is this?" I asked, my voice barely whispering now. "Why are there so many people here?"

No one answered. They just guided me inside. My eyes scanned the room frantically, searching for him—for his smile, for his warm, comforting presence. But he wasn't there. Instead, there was a sea of mourners, their tear-streaked faces turning to look at me, their eyes filled with pity.

I started screaming again. "No! No! He's not dead! He's not! Tobi is not dead!"

They tried to calm me down and hold me, but I shoved them away. "Where is he?!" I demanded. Where is Tobi?!"

And then I saw her. Tobi's mother was standing at the top of the stairs, her face etched with grief, her eyes swollen from crying. She opened her mouth, and the words shattered whatever remained of my world.

"Esther," she said softly, her voice breaking. "He's gone. Tobi is gone."

I shook my head, backing away, my feet stumbling over themselves. "No. No, he's not. He's not gone. He's not. He can't be. He—"

"He's gone, Esther," she repeated, tears streaming down her face. "I didn't want to believe it either, but it's true."

I fell to my knees, the room spinning around me. "No," I whispered, clutching my chest, trying to hold myself together. "No, no, no, no…"

Everything was wrong.

Landing in Abuja and not having Tobi there to pick me up was wrong.

Coming to his family's house and not seeing him there was wrong.

Everything felt like a horrible dream, a nightmare I couldn't wake up from.

Mourners shuffled around, their cries and prayers filling the room, but their voices were just noise, static in my ears. What were they praying for? What were they crying for? What was all this… this **theatre**?

I wanted to scream at them all to stop. To leave me alone and stop saying Tobi's name like he was... like he was gone.

"He's not gone," I muttered to myself. "He's not gone. This is a mistake. They've made a mistake. We need to go. I need to see him. You people should take me to Tobi. Where is he?"

Tobi's aunty put her hand on my shoulder, her touch gentle, but I recoiled as if she had burnt me. "We can't see him now, Esther. You're not in a state—"

"I don't care!" I screamed, my voice raw and broken. "Take me to him! Take me to the mortuary! I need to see him! I need to—"

They tried to calm me down, but I wouldn't hear it. I fought them off, my hands flailing, my breath coming in ragged gasps.

"I need to see him!" I kept screaming. "Take me to him now! I need to see him!"

Eventually, they relented. My brother, his face pale and drawn, agreed, and we were off again, driving through the streets of Abuja, the city a blur outside the window. Two of Tobi's aunties and his uncle came with us. I was shaking, my whole body trembling as if it were going to fall apart.

When we reached the mortuary, I could barely stand. They had to hold me up, one on each side. The smell hit me first—chemical, cold, and metallic. The air was heavy with it. I gagged, my stomach churning, but I didn't care. I needed to see him. I needed to see my Tobi.

"Is that the wife of the deceased?" The attendant asked my brother quietly.

Deceased. The word sent a shiver through me, a sharp stab of pain right to my heart. I shook my head violently. "No," I muttered. "There is no deceased. Nobody is deceased. Tobi is not deceased."

The attendant's eyes softened with pity. He nodded and led us to the cold storage. I watched, my heart in my throat, as they opened the door. The sound of metal scraping against metal made my skin crawl. And then they pulled him out.

Tobi.

My Tobi.

Lying there, so still, so cold. His skin was pale, his eyes closed. He looked like he was sleeping, just sleeping. But he wasn't. I could see it in the stillness of his chest, in the absence of breath.

I screamed. I screamed until my throat was raw, until there was no air left in my lungs. I screamed until I couldn't scream anymore, and then I just stood there, shaking, my eyes locked on him. My husband. My love.

I could see the bruises on his shoulders, the wound on his head. They had covered him up, but I could see. I could see everything.

"Tobi," I whispered, my voice breaking. "Tobi, please… please wake up. Please…"

But he didn't. He just lay there, still and silent, as if he didn't hear me. As if he couldn't.

When they pulled him back into the cold storage, I collapsed against the wall, my body shaking with sobs. My brother tried to pull me away, but I fought him off.

"No!" I screamed. "No, I want to stay! I need to stay! I need to—"

But they wouldn't let me. They dragged me out of the mortuary back to the car. And I screamed the whole way back.

I don't remember getting back to the house. I don't remember much of anything after that. The car ride was a blur, yet the familiar feeling of being in a car stuck with me. Tobi and I had bonded over long drives, discussing our future, dreams, and the life we wanted to build together. The life we thought we had all the time in the world to create. I held onto that feeling in the car, clutching it like a lifeline, desperate to stay afloat amidst the chaos swirling in my mind.

When we pulled up outside the house, I could barely breathe. I turned to everyone in the car and said, "Can you all please leave me? Everyone but my brother." I needed space, air, and Tobi.

I stayed in the car, breathing in and out, trying to find a sliver of peace in the familiar hum of the engine. It wasn't my car, but it was close enough.

God, why him? Why us? Why now?

Why did God give me this love just to snatch it away? Why did He give me Tobi just to take him from me? Why do I lose the men I love?

First, my father, five years ago—five years to the month—and now Tobi. Both of them were in the same damn month. How does God give and take so easily? How does He look down on this earth and rip away everything that means anything to me without even blinking?

Five weeks.

Five weeks after we said our vows.

Five weeks after we promised forever.

How do I even begin again?

They tried to get me to pray—all of them surrounded me, reaching for my hands, urging me to call on God. But I didn't care about prayers. I didn't care about any of it. I wanted to be left alone. The rude shift from congratulations to condolences was jarring. Insane. One minute, they were cheering us on, celebrating us, and now they were all so damn sorry for my loss. It made no sense. I didn't want their food, their drink, their pity. I didn't like the dignitaries flooding in with their practised words and hollow comfort. I didn't believe any of it. I didn't like it. I didn't want anything.

I just wanted to be alone. And no one understood that. No one understood that I didn't want their love, their affection, their pity. I didn't want anything.

I decided to bury him the following week. In Yoruba culture, it's taboo for parents to bury their child, so it all fell on me, the wife, and Temi, his sister. This constant struggle between hope and disbelief was absurd, planning something as final as a burial while still holding on to the desperate, irrational hope that this was all just a cruel joke—that Tobi would wake up, laugh, and we'd go home, and this nightmare would end.

Going back to his house to organise his things and pick out the clothes he would be buried in, I saw his work stuff tossed around. Tobi was always organised. The fact that he had left his things scattered like that was proof he had only meant to be gone briefly.

The chicken stew was still there. Uneaten, in the fridge. I opened it, and the smell hit me like a punch in the gut, knocking the breath out of me. I fell apart right there on the kitchen floor, sobbing and screaming, my body convulsing with the weight of it all. I couldn't do it. I couldn't pack up his life. His suitcase was still out, half-packed for our planned trip—the mattress we had just bought, still fresh and new, untouched by us. My sister, Temi, and Chisom had to take over. I sat there on the floor, useless, paralysed by grief.

The native I had sewn for him, a surprise, ended up being the clothes I chose for him to be buried in. Tobi's church covered the costs of the funeral, but the fact that I was burying him at all felt unreal. I kept waiting for the laughter, for Tobi to just appear and laugh until he cried. I could almost see it, too. He stayed still.

At the service of songs, in the same church where we had given thanks just weeks before, I broke down completely. Seeing his picture up there on the altar sent me spiralling into a grief so deep it felt like I was drowning. But there was something in seeing all those people, all the lives he had touched, all the love and sorrow pouring out for him. People from Korea to Nigeria were shattered beyond belief. It was the only thing that made the grief bearable, seeing how much he had meant to so many. It gave me just enough strength to stand up, speak, and say goodbye.

The next day was the burial. Seeing him in the casket was unreal. I kept waiting for him to rise, get up, laugh, and tell us all that it was a joke, a bad dream. But he didn't. He just lay there, still, cold, gone.

At the cemetery, I went to the ambulance, needing to see him one last time. He lay there, motionless, with the basketball right beside his hands in the overtly padded, lonely casket. I stood there, crying, begging him to wake up, to rise. "Please, Tobi, please. Come back to me. Please."

I screamed until my throat was raw, until my voice gave out. But he didn't move. He didn't make a sound. He didn't wake up. He was gone.

Watching them lower him into the grave was the final blow. I ran to the car, my body heaving with sobs, tears streaming down my face. I cried all the way home.

Tobi was dead.

And I didn't know how to live without him. I didn't know if I could live without him if I even wanted to. In the casket, buried underneath all those layers of dirt, next to my husband, were all the dreams I had dreamed of our future. I saw nothing when I looked into a future without Tobi in it.

WHAT LOVE LEFT UNFINISHED

PIECING TOGETHER A BROKEN HEART WITH THE FRAGMENTS OF US

·······································

Grief was a familiar stranger.

*I*t wrapped around me, heavy and suffocating, its tendrils seeping into every part of my being. In the days after Tobi's death, I came to hate the question: "How are you?" It was a simple phrase, yet it tore at me like a knife.

People asked it with the best intentions, but what did they expect me to say? "I'm fine?" I wasn't fine. I was far from fine. Every time I heard those words, they felt like a cruel joke, an empty gesture that demanded a response I couldn't give. What did they want to hear? That I was surviving? That I was barely keeping my head above water? How do you tell someone that your soul has been hollowed out, that your heart is a gaping wound that bleeds with every breath you take?

Nobody knew what to do with my grief. Not even me.

People still did, even when I told my friends not to ask me how I was doing. They couldn't help themselves, and I understood that. But understanding didn't make it any easier to bear. Even when I was clear about how I wanted to be treated, people tried but often forgot. It was maddening. How was I supposed to be? How was I supposed to breathe, eat, sleep, and continue when my whole world had collapsed? I had just lost my husband, my everything. My beginning and my end.

Chisom stayed with me at the family house, taking care of me as best as possible. My siblings were there too, hovering like satellites, not knowing whether to come closer or to pull away. They meant well, but their presence was suffocating. The funeral was over, and with it, any illusion that this was all a bad dream. It was final. Tobi was gone. He was never coming back. It felt real now, this terrifying emptiness. I was slowly coming to terms with the fact, but where would I go from here? What was I supposed to do?

I didn't know how to move on. I didn't even want to.

There was a Thanksgiving service afterwards. I was numb throughout. People were still visiting, each with a story about

Tobi and a piece of him that they wanted to share with me. It was comforting, in a way, to hear how loved he was and how much he had touched people's lives. But it was also a constant reminder of all that I had lost.

Everyone from all walks of life came, each with their stories and memories. It somehow inspired me and Tobi's father. It made us think about setting up a foundation in Tobi's name to continue his good works and keep his memory alive. It felt right. We registered an NGO in Tobi's honour ASAP, **the Babatobi Ayo Foundation.**

When I finally returned to Lagos, I felt a cold numbness settle over me. I shut myself in my room and cried. I cried until no more tears were left, and then I cried some more. I couldn't look at our wedding pictures. I couldn't look at his pictures. There were some things I mourned more deeply than others. The life we could have had. The children we would never have. The future that had been stolen from us. Looking at his face was too painful.

Weeks later, I decided to return to work. I thought it would help and give me something to focus on, but the first day was horrible. The silence was thick and awkward. People walked on eggshells around me, their pity obvious, their words hesitant. I felt like I was suffocating under their gaze. I couldn't stand it. I caved and left the office, not going back for a while.

When I finally did, everything felt different. Little things were suddenly triggering. Suddenly, people around me were relocating to Canada, announcing their new adventures and fresh starts.

Tobi had his permanent residency, one he would never get to use. It felt like a cruel twist of fate. People were getting married and celebrating anniversaries, and their marriages lasted longer than five weeks. It was hard not to feel robbed, not to be angry. I couldn't deal with the constant reminders of everything I'd lost, everything that had been taken from me. I left work again. I needed to heal, to find some semblance of peace, although people insisted I was making a mistake. They said I needed to keep my mind busy to find a distraction. But how do you distract yourself from a shattered heart?

I failed an exam during that time. It didn't matter. Nothing mattered.

I travelled, seeking the company of friends who knew me well enough to accommodate my grief. I bought random things— Kilishi from the market—and flew to surprise a friend with them in August. She screamed in surprise when she saw me, her eyes wide with shock. "Esther," she said, "is this really you?"

It was as if she didn't expect me to be capable of any kindness or thoughtfulness after all I'd been through. And maybe she was right. But I wanted to feel something, anything other than this numbness that had taken over my soul.

But every time I tried to claw my way back to the surface, grief pulled me under again and again and again. It was a cycle. I would tell myself, *okay, you can function now.* The worst of it is over. Then, I would fall apart again. Then, I would lie to myself again. Rinse and repeat.

The darkness was comforting. Being alone was therapeutic for me. It was easier to stay in bed, to shut out the world and all its noise, than to sit there and listen to everyone tell me how **sorry** they were. "Sorry" was a nothing word, and I was also sick of hearing it. I began to pick up the pieces of my life, little by little. I returned to the gym, pushing myself until my muscles ached and I couldn't think or feel. I began to learn French sometime in October, something I'd always wanted to do but never had the time to learn fully. I had made some attempts before, but now I threw myself into it, spending hours each day conjugating verbs, repeating phrases, anything to keep my mind from spiralling into that dark place.

I learnt French until December.

But in all of this, life just felt vain and pointless. I found myself not wanting anything for myself. Money was meaningless. I started donating all of it to causes I found online, trying to find some purpose, some meaning in the emptiness. When my sister said her mother-in-law wanted to get me something and asked what I wanted, I told her nothing. I told her it was all vanity. She didn't understand, but it didn't matter. I didn't want anything. What could I possibly want now? The one person I wanted to share my life with, share all the things with, was gone. What was the point of accumulating possessions when anyone at any time could just be so permanently gone?

People in my life were worried for me, but I was determined to find my way to heal. I needed to do it my way. After all, the person I wanted to share everything with was dead.

The Babatobi Ayo Foundation launched in September 2023. The foundation was set up to continue Tobi's legacy and fund the causes he stood for. Tobi was very passionate about basketball, especially the FCT Basketball Team he coached until his death. In fact, the team won a game the day before his death, and he was interviewed on national TV because of that feat.

Tobi also paid school fees for several people and gave to a number of causes, most of whom couldn't afford basic necessities. Most of the causes he gave to were unknown to us until after his death when the beneficiaries informed us about what he used to do for them.

Tobi was also a children's teacher at his church, First Baptist Church, Garki. In light of this, the foundation also sponsors **Vacation Bible School**, which usually resumes during summer when children are on break.

The support was overwhelming. So many people who loved Tobi and wanted to keep his memory alive came. It was a beautiful thing to see how much he had touched people's lives. An outpouring of love that day buoyed me and gave me the courage to speak. I stood there in front of all those people, and I felt a flicker of hope for the first time. Maybe there was a way forward. Perhaps I could find a way to live with this pain.

Life can be so funny at times. September was finally here. It was the month I was supposed to have moved in with Tobi, but here I was surrounded by people wearing the branded foundation shirts, a foundation that came about as a result of his death. There would not be any moving happening, and there was no marital bliss.

Someone asked me, "Knowing what you know now, would you have still married Tobi?"

"Yes," I said without hesitation. "I would have."

Because even though the pain was unbearable, even though the grief was overwhelming, loving Tobi was the best thing that ever happened to me, and I wouldn't trade that for anything in the world. Not even for a moment.

I closed my eyes, letting his memories wash over me. I could still see his smile, hear his laughter, feel his hand in mine. I held onto those memories like a lifeline, like a beacon guiding me through the storm. I knew the road ahead would be long and hard, that there would be more dark days than light, but for the first time since his death, I felt a spark of hope. I knew it would be a while, though, before those memories stopped feeling like a razor to my heart.

I knew that, somehow, I would find my way through this. I would find a way to live again.

And I knew that Tobi would be with me every step of the way.

Because love, true love, never really dies. It lives on in the people we touch, in the lives we change, and in the hearts we hold. And Tobi had touched so many lives and changed so many hearts, including mine.

So, I held onto that, the love and the memories. And I took a deep breath and took the first step forward into the unknown, into the future, into a life without Tobi.

I knew, somehow, that I would be healed.

I would find a way to keep living, loving, and moving forward. I knew that I needed to give myself time to feel this grief—time to digest, understand, and feel all the fickle feelings. How much pushing aside could I do before I fell apart again? I had to try to heal myself.

For Tobi.

For myself.

For all the people who loved him and missed him.

Because that's what he would have wanted.

And that's what I would do.

I would keep going.

One step at a time.

One day at a time.

Until the pain was no longer a constant ache, and the memories brought more smiles than tears.

Until I could remember Tobi, not with sadness, but with joy.

Because that's how he would want to be remembered.

With love.

With joy.

With a heart full of hope.

And that's what I would do.

For him.

For us.

For the life we had.

The life that had been stolen from us.

WHAT LOVE LEFT UNFINISHED

THE LIGHT
THAT REMAINS
SHINES

....

The essence of our chanced encounter...

The experience with Tobi transformed the very essence of who I was. I realised we had crammed a lifetime of love into our brief time. It was a whirlwind of emotions but also the most beautiful chapter of my life. The love we shared, though brief, was infinite in its depth. I am who I am today because of Tobi.

The foundation we started in his honour is flourishing, funding his basketball players and team, touching lives just as he did. When I see those boys on the court, I see Tobi in them. I see his passion, drive, and love for the game and life. It brings a bittersweet smile to my face, knowing that his legacy lives on in the hearts of so many. Admitting the pain was the first step to healing. I remember the moment I finally allowed myself to feel it, to really feel it. I had been pushing it away, trying to stay strong for everyone else, but I realised I needed to be strong for myself, too. I needed to face the pain head-on, to let it wash over me like a tidal wave, to let it break me down so I could start to rebuild.

I threw myself into learning French. It was something that required all of my focus, something that allowed me to escape, if only for a little while. I found myself chattering about it non-stop to anyone who would listen. It was freeing to be in a new space, a new headspace, where no one knew me or my story. There were no pitying stares or worried glances. For a few moments, I could just be Esther, the woman who was learning a new language and finding joy in something again—not Esther, the woman with the dead husband.

That was also the first time I didn't fall apart on the fifth of the month like I had done every month after Tobi's death. Every month, like clockwork, the grief would hit me anew, a fresh wave of pain that left me gasping for breath. But not that month. That month, I felt a small flicker of hope. Maybe, just maybe, I was starting to heal.

By November, Tobi's parents visited, and I drove them around. We celebrated Tobi's mother's birthday. I surprised her with a cake, and we celebrated, even when the tears came. But they were healing tears. Seeing them smile and laugh healed a part of me, too. I realised how privileged I was to have married into such a wonderful family. They had become my family, and in them, I found a piece of Tobi that I could hold onto.

As December approached, I found myself dreading the holidays. The thought of spending December alone filled me with a deep sense of dread. I worried if I should travel and get away from the memories that haunted me at every turn. But the thought of travelling alone was depressing, and so was the thought of sitting alone in my apartment, surrounded by memories of Tobi.

I decided to stay in Nigeria and face my fears. A friend, Jojo, was getting married, but I was still determining if I would be strong enough to attend. Weddings were hard now, a painful reminder of what I had lost. But I booked my flight anyway, without knowing how to get from the airport to Tobi's family house. As I boarded the flight, my phone buzzed with a text from my friend, Katelem: "See you soon."

I realised then that I had been blessed with amazing friends. How did he know? How did he always seem to know what I needed, even when I didn't?

When I arrived, I was welcomed warmly. Tobi's dad showed me a tribute he had made to Tobi in the backyard. It had Tobi's nickname, **T50**. I felt a lump form in my throat, tears welling up in my eyes. "He would have loved this," I whispered, my voice choking with emotion.

"We miss him every day," Tobi's dad said, his voice soft. "But he's still with us in everything we do."

I nodded, unable to speak. The tears flowed freely now, but they were not tears of despair. They were tears of love, of remembrance.

I attended the wedding, but it wasn't easy. From the moment I walked in, I felt out of place, like I was intruding on a world that no longer felt like mine. The joy, laughter, and celebration were all so foreign to me now. It was hard to focus on the ceremony, my mind drifting to my wedding day, the vows Tobi and I had exchanged, and the love that had filled every corner of the room. The tears that threatened to fall were a constant reminder of what I had lost.

Staying to the end felt like a battle with myself. I fought the urge to leave, to run away from all the memories. I wanted to be happy for my friend and celebrate her joy, but every smile felt like betrayal and forced. I felt so empty inside.

And then there were the men. Being hit on was uncomfortable. It annoyed me because I knew they would not approach me if Tobi was here.

I wanted to scream at them, to tell them they didn't understand or couldn't possibly understand. How could I move on when a part of me was still deeply rooted in my love for Tobi? Their advances, their attempts at flirtation, made my skin crawl. I wasn't ready for this, for any of it. I was still trying to figure out how to live in a world without him, how to breathe without him by my side.

Even getting an Uber at the end of the night was a challenge. I stood outside, my phone in hand, staring at the app but unable to bring myself to press the button. The thought of getting into a stranger's car, of sitting in the back seat alone, filled me with dread. If Tobi were here, I wouldn't need an Uber. He would have been there with me, holding my hand, guiding me through the crowd, making sure I was okay.

The next day, I went to a friend's place but often found myself at Tobi's family house. They were my safe space now, the only place I felt less lost.

Christmas Day was the hardest. I cried my eyes out, thinking of the plans Tobi and I had made and our dreams. Seeing all the lovey-dovey couples was like a knife to my heart.

I was alone, but I wrote about my feelings and posted them on Medium. It was therapeutic, in a way. *Healing is a lonely road.* Everyone has their own lives, their own families, their own joys. But mine, the person I wanted to share my life with, was gone.

Christmas was harder than I had anticipated. Everything screamed Tobi. I missed him everywhere. The conversations, the food, the laughter—all of it reminded me of him. We tried to keep the cheer, but it was hard. I spent a lot of time with Tobi's parents. They were my anchor, the only thing keeping me grounded.

By the New Year, I decided to resume work. I was determined not to hear any more, "It's the New Year; move on." I wanted to move on, but grief doesn't work like that. It doesn't follow a timeline. Resuming work was better than before, but it was still hard. I slowly acclimatised to the work environment and began to find my footing again.

The year ahead felt daunting. How would I get through another year without Tobi? But time marches on, even when I am afraid.

Time moved, and I began to heal.

It has been a year since Tobi died. We recently held Tobi's first-year memorial. In the days following, I felt a huge burden lifted off my shoulders. The past year had been filled with so many firsts that terrified me—the first wedding anniversary without him, the first birthday without him, the first anniversary of his death. But each of these firsts has passed, and I have found myself stronger on the other side, still standing.

One of the things that has helped me through the grief is writing on Medium. It has become my outlet, my way of making sense of the pain. Over time, I have grown a family and a following there, people reaching out to tell me how much my story has touched them. I have shared my rawest moments, my deepest fears, and my journey through grief. I have bared my soul to strangers, and in doing so, I have found connection, understanding, and support. It is surreal when people recognise me from Medium or approach my brother to ask if he is related to "Esther from Medium." I never imagined my words could resonate deeply with others, but they have.

Another source of comfort was a sermon from Apostle Joshua Selman. He preached it the day before Tobi died, and I resisted watching it for so long. A neighbour of Tobi's, Mrs. Kolawole, had recommended it, insisting it would bring me peace, but I couldn't bring myself to watch it.

Finally, one night, I fell asleep while watching it with my sister. When I woke up, my sister insisted I finish it. I felt seen, heard, and understood for the first time as I watched. The words spoke directly to my pain, offering me solace in a way nothing else had. On hard days, I still watch that sermon and other related ones. They have become a balm for my wounded heart, a source of strength when I feel I have none left.

Tobi's pastor, Pastor Tom, has also been a pillar of support throughout this journey. Not only did the church cover all the expenses for Tobi's funeral, but the pastor has consistently made time for me because of his love for Tobi. He is always willing to listen, offer a shoulder to cry on, and provide guidance when I feel lost. Many people who loved Tobi have extended that love to me, enveloping me in a cocoon of care and compassion.

Through all of this, I have learnt that grief is not linear. There are good days and bad days, moments of joy interspersed with moments of sorrow. But I have also learnt that it is okay to feel both. It is okay to find happiness again, laugh, love, and live. Tobi would have wanted that for me. He would have wanted me to continue living and finding beauty in the world, even in his absence.

The love we shared will always be a part of me. It has shaped, moulded, and made me who I am today. I carry Tobi with me in everything I do, every decision I make, and every step I take. His light continues to shine through me, guiding, comforting, and reminding me that love is eternal.

As I look ahead, I know there will be challenges. There will be moments when the grief feels too heavy to bear, when the memories come rushing back, and the pain feels fresh all over again. But I also know that I am strong. I have survived the darkest days and will continue to find my way through the light.

And so, I move forward, one step at a time, one day at a time. Life goes on, and so will I—for Tobi, for myself, and for all the people who love me and need me.

Because love never really dies. It lives on in the people we touch, the lives we change, and the hearts we hold. I will hold onto that love, that memory, that hope.

I will keep going. Because completing love's task is what I'm meant to do.

I am Esther, and this is my story—a story of love, loss, healing, and hope—a story that is still being written, one day at a time.

WHAT LOVE LEFT UNFINISHED

MY MUSIC PLAYLIST

Music was a source of comfort during this phase, so I thought it would be nice to share some of the soundtracks that have helped me to this day. Enjoy.

- "Fear Is Not My Future" - Todd Galberth feat. Tasha Cobbs Leonard

- "God Will Work It Out" - Maverick City Music feat. Naomi Raine & Israel Houghton

- "It Is Well" - Kristene DiMarco

- "My Life Is in Your Hands" - Maverick City Music feat. Chandler Moore

- "Promises" - Maverick City Music feat. Naomi Raine & Joe L. Barnes

- "In Christ Alone" - Don Moen

- "He Never Sleeps" - Don Moen

- "Joy in the Morning" - Tauren Wells

- "Still/Be Still and Know (Medley)" - Don Moen

- "My Heart Will Trust" - Hillsong Worship

- "God Will Make a Way" - Don Moen

- "In Jesus Name (God of Possible)" - Don Moen

CONNECT WITH ME

Instagram: @estherokuru
Twitter: @stargirl_Okuru
Facebook: Okuru Esther
LinkedIn: Esther Okuru

Scan here to read more stories from me on Medium.

www.ingramcontent.com/pod-product-compliance
Lightning Source LLC
Chambersburg PA
CBHW022006310125
21191CB00012B/838